AWS Certified Developer Associate Step by Step Certification Study Guide, to Pass the Developers Exam With Confidence

Table of Contents

Introduction

Welcome to the world of AWS Certified Developer! If you're reading this introduction, you've likely embarked on a journey to become an AWS Certified Developer, a credential that showcases your expertise in designing, building, and maintaining applications on the Amazon Web Services (AWS) platform. Congratulations on taking this significant step towards advancing your career in cloud computing.

In today's rapidly evolving technology landscape, cloud computing is at the forefront of innovation. AWS, as a leading cloud service provider, empowers businesses and individuals to harness the power of the cloud to create scalable, secure, and efficient applications. The AWS Certified Developer certification is a highly regarded validation of your skills and knowledge in developing applications on the AWS platform.

This book, "AWS Certified Developer Practice Test: Questions, Answers, and Exam Success," has been meticulously crafted to aid you in your journey towards AWS Developer certification. Whether you are a seasoned developer looking to validate your skills or someone starting fresh in the world of cloud computing, this resource is designed to be your trusted companion.

In this book, you will find a comprehensive collection of practice questions that closely mimic the format and difficulty level of the actual AWS Certified Developer – Associate exam. Each question has been carefully crafted to assess your understanding of key AWS services, best practices, and developer tools.

To maximize your learning experience, each practice question is accompanied by a detailed explanation of the correct answer. This not only helps you identify the correct responses but also provides valuable insights into why those answers are correct. Additionally, you will find references to AWS documentation and resources for further study, ensuring you have a well-rounded understanding of the exam topics.

To make the most of this resource, consider the following study approach:

Diagnostic Assessment: Begin by taking a diagnostic assessment to gauge your current knowledge and identify areas where you need improvement.

Focused Study: Review the explanations provided for each practice question, paying close attention to the AWS services and concepts being tested.

Supplemental Resources: Use the recommended AWS documentation and resources to deepen your understanding of specific topics.

Timed Practice Tests: As you progress, take full-length timed practice tests to simulate the exam environment and assess your readiness.

Review and Repeat: Continue practicing and reviewing until you consistently achieve passing scores on practice tests.

Exam Day: On the day of the exam, approach it with confidence, knowing that you have thoroughly prepared by using this book as a valuable resource.

The journey to becoming an AWS Certified Developer is both challenging and rewarding. It demonstrates your commitment to staying at the forefront of cloud technology and opens doors to exciting career opportunities. This book aims to be your trusted companion on this journey, providing you with the knowledge, practice, and confidence you need to excel in the exam.

As you embark on this learning adventure, remember that success is not solely measured by passing the exam but also by the skills and expertise you acquire along the way. The AWS Certified Developer certification is a testament to your dedication to excellence in cloud development.

So, let's get started! Dive into the practice questions, absorb the explanations, and embrace the opportunity to become an AWS Certified Developer. Your success awaits, and this book is here to guide you every step of the way. Good luck!

1. Introduction to AWS Certification

Understanding the AWS Certified Developer Certification

In the dynamic landscape of cloud computing, Amazon Web Services (AWS) stands out as a frontrunner, offering a vast array of services and solutions to individuals and organizations worldwide. AWS has revolutionized the way we build, deploy, and scale applications, making it a dominant force in the industry. To prove your competence in harnessing the power of AWS for application development, the AWS Certified Developer certification is your ticket to recognition and credibility.

Why AWS Certification Matters

The AWS Certified Developer certification is one of the most sought-after credentials in the IT industry, and for good reason. It serves as a testament to your expertise in developing applications on the AWS platform. Here are some compelling reasons why AWS certification matters:

1. Validation of Skills: AWS certifications are recognized globally as a benchmark of excellence. Achieving certification demonstrates that you possess the skills and knowledge required to design, build, and maintain applications on AWS.

2. Career Advancement: AWS-certified professionals are in high demand. Holding an AWS certification can open doors to new job opportunities and increase your earning potential. It also allows you to stand out in a competitive job market.

3. Enhanced Confidence: Certification not only boosts your professional credibility but also instills confidence in your abilities. It reassures both employers and clients that you can effectively work with AWS services and technologies.

4. Access to Exclusive Resources: AWS offers a range of exclusive resources to certified professionals, including access to the AWS Certified Global Community, which provides networking opportunities, insights, and the latest updates in the AWS ecosystem.

5. Keeping Pace with Innovation: AWS continually introduces new services and features. Maintaining your certification requires you to stay current with the latest advancements in cloud technology, ensuring that your skills remain relevant.

The AWS Certified Developer - Associate Exam

The AWS Certified Developer - Associate certification is specifically designed for individuals who want to demonstrate their proficiency in developing applications on the

AWS platform. To earn this certification, you must pass the AWS Certified Developer - Associate exam, which is challenging but achievable with the right preparation.

Key Exam Details:

Exam Code: DVA-C01

Prerequisite: AWS recommends having at least one year of hands-on experience with AWS services and a strong understanding of at least one high-level programming language.

Exam Format: The exam consists of multiple-choice and multiple-response questions. You have 130 minutes to complete the exam, and the passing score is set by AWS.

Exam Domains:

The AWS Certified Developer - Associate exam covers a range of domains, each with its own set of topics. These domains include:

Deployment: In this domain, you'll be tested on your ability to deploy applications using AWS services like Elastic Beanstalk, Lambda, and CloudFormation.

Security: This domain assesses your knowledge of AWS Identity and Access Management (IAM), security best practices, and encryption mechanisms.

Development with AWS Services: Here, you'll be quizzed on your proficiency with AWS services like DynamoDB, S3, and API Gateway, and how to integrate them into applications.

Refactoring: This domain focuses on your ability to optimize existing code for AWS and troubleshoot applications using CloudWatch.

Monitoring and Troubleshooting: You'll need to demonstrate your skills in monitoring AWS resources and effectively troubleshooting issues in this domain.

Preparing for Success

Preparing for the AWS Certified Developer - Associate exam requires dedication and a structured approach to learning. This book is your companion on this journey, offering a comprehensive collection of practice questions, answers, and explanations to help you solidify your knowledge and build confidence.

In the following chapters, you'll delve into the intricacies of AWS services, developer tools, and best practices. With each practice question, you'll not only test your understanding but also gain valuable insights into the world of AWS development.

The AWS Certified Developer certification is your gateway to a world of exciting opportunities in cloud development. So, let's embark on this journey together, one chapter at a time, and work toward achieving your AWS certification goals. Remember, the sky's the limit when you're powered by AWS!

The Importance of Practice Tests in Exam Preparation

Exam preparation can be a challenging and often daunting process. Whether you're studying for a school exam, a professional certification, or any other type of assessment, practice tests are a valuable tool that should not be overlooked. They play a crucial role in helping you achieve success, and here's why:

1. Assessment of Knowledge

Practice tests allow you to assess your current level of knowledge and understanding of the subject matter. By attempting questions similar to those you'll encounter on the actual exam, you can gauge where you stand in terms of readiness. This assessment helps you identify your strengths and weaknesses, providing a clear picture of what areas need more attention.

2. Familiarity with Exam Format

Exams come in various formats, such as multiple-choice, essay questions, or practical exercises. Practice tests mimic the format of the real exam, helping you become familiar with its structure and requirements. This familiarity can reduce anxiety and boost your confidence when you sit for the actual test.

3. Time Management Skills

Time management is a critical skill when taking any exam. Practice tests enforce time constraints, forcing you to answer questions within a specific timeframe. Practicing under time pressure helps you develop effective time management strategies and ensures that you can complete the exam within the allocated period.

4. Identifying Weak Areas

Practice tests reveal which specific topics or concepts you find challenging. Once you identify these weak areas, you can dedicate more time and effort to studying and reviewing them. This targeted approach is more efficient than studying everything uniformly.

5. Building Confidence

Confidence plays a significant role in exam success. As you practice and become more comfortable with the material and the exam format, your confidence will grow. Confidence can help you stay calm during the exam and make better decisions when answering questions.

6. Reducing Test Anxiety

Exam anxiety is common and can negatively impact performance. Regularly practicing with mock exams helps reduce test anxiety because it desensitizes you to the stress associated with taking a test. You become more accustomed to the exam environment and the pressure it entails.

7. Measuring Progress

Practice tests are like milestones on your journey to exam readiness. They allow you to track your progress over time. As you take multiple practice tests and see your scores improve, you'll gain a sense of accomplishment and motivation to continue working towards your goal.

8. Reinforcing Learning

Repetition is a powerful learning tool. When you repeatedly encounter and answer questions related to the subject matter, you reinforce your understanding of the material. This helps you retain information and recall it more easily during the actual exam.

9. Strategic Exam Strategy Development

Through practice tests, you can develop and refine your exam-taking strategies. For example, you can experiment with strategies like answering easier questions first, flagging challenging ones for later review, and budgeting your time wisely.

10. Realistic Simulation

Practice tests aim to create a realistic simulation of the actual exam experience. This includes not only the format and content but also the conditions like sitting for a fixed duration in an exam-like environment. This realism prepares you mentally for what to expect on the big day.

Practice tests are an integral part of effective exam preparation. They provide you with insights into your knowledge, help you manage time efficiently, boost confidence, and ultimately increase your chances of success. Therefore, when preparing for an exam, make practice tests a fundamental component of your study plan. They can be the key to unlocking your full potential and achieving the results you desire.

Setting Clear Goals for Certification Success

Certification exams are not just tests of knowledge; they are stepping stones toward career advancement, personal growth, and professional recognition. To maximize your chances of success in your certification journey, it's crucial to set clear, well-defined goals. These goals will serve as your roadmap, helping you stay motivated, focused, and organized throughout your preparation. Here's how to set and achieve clear goals for certification success:

1. Choose the Right Certification

Start by carefully selecting the certification that aligns with your career aspirations and interests. Research the available certifications, their prerequisites, and the skills they validate. Ensure that the certification you choose is relevant to your current job or the job you aspire to have.

2. Define Your "Why"

Clearly articulate why you want to earn this certification. Understand the specific benefits it will bring to your career and personal development. Having a compelling reason behind your goal will provide the motivation needed to overcome challenges and stay committed.

3. Set Specific, Measurable, Achievable, Relevant, and Time-bound (SMART) Goals

Use the SMART framework to structure your goals:

Specific: Define your goal as precisely as possible. For example, "I want to achieve AWS Certified Solutions Architect - Associate certification."

Measurable: Determine how you will measure your progress. This could be through practice test scores, completion of study materials, or a target exam date.

Achievable: Ensure that your goal is realistic and attainable given your current circumstances, resources, and time constraints.

Relevant: Ensure that your goal aligns with your career and personal aspirations. It should be something that genuinely matters to you.

Time-bound: Set a clear deadline for when you intend to achieve your certification. This creates a sense of urgency and helps you stay on track.

4. Break Down Your Goal

Large certification goals can feel overwhelming. Break them down into smaller, manageable milestones. For example, if your ultimate goal is to pass a certification exam, break it down into studying specific topics, completing practice tests, and scheduling the exam.

5. Create a Study Plan

Develop a comprehensive study plan that outlines what you need to study, when you will study, and how you will measure your progress. Allocate specific time slots for studying in your daily or weekly schedule.

6. Utilize Available Resources

Identify the study materials, courses, books, and practice tests that will help you prepare effectively. Take advantage of online courses, textbooks, official study guides, and reputable practice test providers.

7. Practice Regularly

Practice is essential for exam success. Regularly take practice tests to assess your knowledge, identify weak areas, and get comfortable with the exam format. Use the results to adapt your study plan as needed.

8. Seek Support and Accountability

Share your goals with a mentor, study group, or friend who can provide support and hold you accountable. Discussing your progress and challenges with others can be motivating and help you stay on track.

9. Stay Adaptable

Be open to adjusting your goals and study plan as circumstances change. Life can be unpredictable, so flexibility is essential. If you encounter unexpected challenges, such as work demands or personal issues, don't be discouraged. Adjust your timeline and keep moving forward.

10. Stay Persistent and Positive

Certification journeys can be demanding, but persistence is key. Stay focused on your "why," remind yourself of your goals regularly, and maintain a positive mindset. Celebrate small victories along the way to stay motivated.

11. Track Your Progress

Regularly review your progress against your SMART goals. Celebrate your achievements and use any setbacks as opportunities for learning and growth.

12. Schedule Your Exam

Once you feel confident in your preparation and consistently perform well on practice tests, schedule your certification exam. Having a concrete exam date can provide additional motivation and a clear target to work toward.

Setting clear goals for certification success is an integral part of your journey. It not only keeps you on track but also ensures that your efforts are focused and purposeful. By following these steps and staying committed to your goals, you'll be well-prepared to achieve certification success and reap the benefits it brings to your career and personal growth.

2. AWS Certified Developer Deployment Questions and Answers

Questions

A firm wants to use Amazon API Gateway to enable authentication for its new REST service. Each request must include HTTP headers with a client ID and user ID to authenticate the calls. The authentication data in an Amazon DynamoDB table must be compared to these credentials. What must the organization do in order to establish API Gateway authentication?

A. Create an AWS Lambda authorizer that uses the DynamoDB authentication table as a reference.

B. Make a model that needs the credentials, then provide API Gateway access to the authentication database.

C. Require credentials in integration requests, then grant API Gateway access to the authentication table.

D. Create an Amazon Cognito authorizer that uses the DynamoDB authentication database as a reference.

Which AWS service can be used to easily deploy and manage containerized applications?

A. Amazon EC2

B. AWS Elastic Beanstalk

C. Amazon ECS

D. AWS Lambda

What is the primary benefit of using AWS Elastic Beanstalk for deploying applications?

A. Fine-grained control over infrastructure configuration.

B. Simplified application deployment and management.

C. Reduced cost compared to other deployment options.

D. Automatic load balancing and scaling.

In the context of AWS Elastic Beanstalk, what is a "platform"?

A. The physical data center where your application runs.

B. A predefined runtime environment with a specific configuration.

C. The software development framework used by your application.

D. The network architecture of your application.

When using AWS Elastic Beanstalk, what is the purpose of an environment?

A. To define the physical hardware specifications of your application.

B. To manage the deployment of application versions and instances.

C. To store and retrieve configuration settings for your application.

D. To monitor and troubleshoot application performance.

Which AWS service is designed for building and running serverless applications?

A. Amazon EC2

B. Amazon RDS

C. AWS Lambda

D. Amazon S3

In AWS Lambda, what is the maximum amount of memory that can be allocated to a function?

A. 512 MB

B. 1 GB

C. 2 GB

D. 3 GB

What is an AWS CloudFormation stack?

A. A collection of virtual servers in the AWS cloud.

B. A version control repository for AWS resources.

C. A template for creating AWS resources in a specified order.

D. A group of IAM roles associated with an AWS account.

Which AWS service can be used to manage and provision resources through code, allowing for infrastructure as code (IAC)?

A. AWS CloudFormation

B. AWS Elastic Beanstalk

C. Amazon S3

D. Amazon RDS

What is the purpose of an Amazon CloudWatch alarm?

A. To create an instance of an EC2 server.

B. To monitor and take automated actions based on predefined thresholds.

C. To store log data from AWS services.

D. To provision resources in a VPC.

Which AWS service can be used to deploy a web application with serverless architecture, allowing developers to focus on code without managing infrastructure?

A. AWS Elastic Beanstalk

B. Amazon EC2

C. AWS Lambda

D. Amazon RDS

What is an Amazon Elastic Container Service (Amazon ECS) task definition?

A. A script for configuring EC2 instances.

B. A blueprint for creating a Docker container.

C. A template for defining how a container should run.

D. A security group for managing network access.

When deploying a new version of an application with AWS Elastic Beanstalk, what happens to the previous environment?

A. It is automatically deleted.

B. It remains running alongside the new environment.

C. It is paused until the new environment is stable.

D. It is terminated after the new environment is deployed successfully.

What is the purpose of Amazon API Gateway?

A. To provide a graphical user interface for managing AWS resources.

B. To manage API keys for accessing AWS services.

C. To create, publish, and manage APIs for applications.

D. To host static websites and web applications.

What AWS service can be used to automate the deployment of applications in a continuous integration and continuous deployment (CI/CD) pipeline?

A. AWS Elastic Beanstalk

B. AWS Lambda

C. AWS CodePipeline

D. Amazon S3

In AWS Elastic Beanstalk, what is the primary role of an environment tier?

A. To specify the number of instances for the environment.

B. To define the environment's security groups and IAM roles.

C. To categorize environments based on their purpose and resources.

D. To configure the environment's network settings and VPC.

Which AWS service is used to deploy code and automate application releases?

A. AWS Elastic Beanstalk

B. AWS Lambda

C. AWS CodeDeploy

D. Amazon ECS

In the context of AWS Elastic Beanstalk, what is a "solution stack"?

A. A collection of software components that make up an application.

B. A predefined set of AWS resources used for deploying an application.

C. A group of Amazon RDS instances that store application data.

D. A list of IAM policies associated with an AWS user.

What is the primary function of AWS CloudFormation?

A. To provide access to a centralized log management service.

B. To automate the provisioning and management of AWS resources.

C. To optimize the performance of AWS services.

D. To facilitate real-time communication between AWS services.

Which AWS service can be used to monitor the performance of AWS resources and applications?

A. Amazon RDS

B. Amazon S3

C. Amazon CloudWatch

D. Amazon VPC

How does AWS Lambda pricing work?

A. Pay per minute of compute time used.

B. Pay a fixed monthly fee regardless of usage.

C. Pay per API request made to the Lambda function.

D. Pay a fixed annual subscription fee.

What is the primary purpose of AWS Elastic Beanstalk environments?

A. To group similar AWS resources together for billing purposes.

B. To define the runtime configuration for an application.

C. To provide a secure network environment for AWS resources.

D. To manage the geographical distribution of an application.

In AWS Lambda, what is the maximum execution timeout for a function?

A. 5 seconds

B. 1 minute

C. 15 minutes

D. 24 hours

What is the purpose of AWS Elastic Beanstalk application versions?

A. To specify the number of EC2 instances in an environment.

B. To define the programming languages used in an application.

C. To track and manage changes to the application's code and configuration.

D. To control access to AWS resources.

Which AWS service can be used to automate the deployment of code to multiple environments, such as development, testing, and production?

A. AWS Elastic Beanstalk

B. AWS Lambda

C. AWS CodePipeline

D. Amazon EC2 Auto Scaling

What is an AWS Lambda function?

A. A virtual server that runs in the AWS cloud.

B. A containerized application that can be deployed on AWS.

C. A piece of code that can be executed in response to events.

D. A relational database service provided by AWS.

How can you enable versioning for an Amazon S3 bucket?

A. By creating a new bucket for each version of an object.

B. By enabling the "Versioning" option for the bucket.

C. By using AWS CloudFormation templates.

D. By configuring a lifecycle policy for the bucket.

What AWS service can be used to manage and store container images for services like Amazon ECS?

A. Amazon S3

B. Amazon EC2

C. Amazon ECR

D. AWS Lambda

Which AWS service can be used to automate the provisioning and management of infrastructure using code?

A. Amazon EC2

B. Amazon RDS

C. AWS CloudFormation

D. AWS Lambda

In AWS Elastic Beanstalk, what is the purpose of an environment URL?

A. To specify the geographic region in which an environment is hosted.

B. To provide a public web address for accessing the application.

C. To define the database connection string for the environment.

D. To configure environment-specific security settings.

Answers

Here are the answers to the questions:

Answer: A

Explanation: To establish API Gateway authentication with custom credentials stored in Amazon DynamoDB, you can create an AWS Lambda authorizer. This Lambda function can validate the HTTP headers containing client IDs and user IDs against the data in the DynamoDB authentication table. The Lambda authorizer allows you to customize the authentication logic and interact with various AWS services like DynamoDB to validate credentials.

Answer: C

Explanation: Amazon Elastic Container Service (Amazon ECS) is designed for deploying and managing containerized applications. It provides an orchestration service for Docker containers, making it easier to manage and scale containerized applications.

Answer: B

Explanation: AWS Elastic Beanstalk simplifies application deployment and management by abstracting away the underlying infrastructure details. It provides an easy-to-use platform for deploying and scaling applications, allowing developers to focus on writing code rather than managing infrastructure.

Answer: B

Explanation: In AWS Elastic Beanstalk, a "platform" refers to a predefined runtime environment with a specific configuration. It includes the operating system, web server, and other software components needed to run an application. Developers can choose a platform that suits their application's requirements.

Answer: B

Explanation: An AWS Elastic Beanstalk environment is a collection of AWS resources (EC2 instances, RDS databases, etc.) that run an application version. It includes configuration settings, such as environment variables, and can be categorized into different tiers (e.g., web server environment, worker environment) based on its purpose and resources.

Answer: C

Explanation: AWS Lambda is designed for building and running serverless applications. It allows developers to run code in response to events without managing servers. AWS Lambda automatically scales based on the number of requests and provides a cost-effective way to build highly scalable and event-driven applications.

Answer: C

Explanation: In AWS Lambda, the maximum amount of memory that can be allocated to a function is 3 GB. This memory allocation determines the CPU power and network bandwidth available to the function during execution.

Answer: C

Explanation: An AWS CloudFormation stack is a collection of AWS resources that you can manage as a single unit. It is defined by a CloudFormation template, which specifies the AWS resources and their configuration. Stacks make it easier to create, update, and delete groups of related AWS resources in a coordinated manner.

Answer: A

Explanation: AWS CloudFormation is used to manage and provision AWS resources through code (Infrastructure as Code - IAC). It allows you to define the desired state of your infrastructure using templates, making it easier to create and manage resources consistently.

Answer: B

Explanation: An Amazon CloudWatch alarm is used to monitor AWS resources and take automated actions based on predefined thresholds. For example, you can create an alarm to trigger a notification or auto-scaling action when a certain metric exceeds a specified threshold.

Answer: D

Explanation: Amazon API Gateway is designed for creating, publishing, and managing APIs for applications. It can be used to build serverless applications using AWS Lambda, allowing developers to focus on code without managing infrastructure.

Answer: C

Explanation: An Amazon Elastic Container Service (Amazon ECS) task definition is a template that describes how a container should run, including container image, CPU, memory requirements, and networking settings. It is used to define how containers are launched within Amazon ECS clusters.

Answer: B

Explanation: When deploying a new version of an application with AWS Elastic Beanstalk, the previous environment remains running alongside the new environment. This allows for easy rollback in case of issues with the new version. However, the old environment can be terminated if it is no longer needed.

Answer: C

Explanation: The primary purpose of Amazon API Gateway is to create, publish, and manage APIs for applications. It acts as a gateway that enables developers to expose APIs to clients, including mobile apps and web applications.

Answer: C

Explanation: AWS CodePipeline is used to automate the deployment of code in a continuous integration and continuous deployment (CI/CD) pipeline. It allows you to define and automate the stages of your software release process.

Answer: B

Explanation: In AWS Elastic Beanstalk, an environment tier defines the runtime configuration for an application. It specifies the infrastructure resources, such as instance types and autoscaling settings, used by the environment.

Answer: C

Explanation: AWS CodeDeploy is used to deploy code and automate application releases. It allows you to define deployment strategies, rollbacks, and automation scripts for deploying code to various environments.

Answer: B

Explanation: In the context of AWS Elastic Beanstalk, a "solution stack" refers to a predefined set of AWS resources used for deploying an application. It includes the runtime environment, web server, and other components required to run the application.

Answer: B

Explanation: The primary function of AWS CloudFormation is to automate the provisioning and management of AWS resources through templates. It allows you to define and deploy infrastructure as code (IAC) using JSON or YAML templates.

Answer: C

Explanation: Amazon CloudWatch is used to monitor the performance of AWS resources and applications. It collects and tracks metrics, sets alarms, and provides insights into resource utilization and application health.

Answer: A

Explanation: AWS Lambda pricing is based on the amount of compute time used. You pay for the number of milliseconds your code executes and the amount of memory allocated to the function.

Answer: B

Explanation: AWS Elastic Beanstalk environments are used to define the runtime configuration for an application. They specify the resources, including EC2 instances, used by the application. The environment tier categorizes environments based on their purpose and resources.

Answer: C

Explanation: In AWS Lambda, the maximum execution timeout for a function is 15 minutes. Functions are terminated if they run for longer than this timeout period.

Answer: C

Explanation: AWS Elastic Beanstalk application versions are used to track and manage changes to the application's code and configuration. They allow you to deploy, rollback, and manage different versions of your application.

Answer: C

Explanation: AWS CodePipeline is used to automate the deployment of code to multiple environments, such as development, testing, and production. It provides a continuous integration and continuous deployment (CI/CD) pipeline for managing software releases.

Answer: C

Explanation: An AWS Lambda function is a piece of code that can be executed in response to events. It is a serverless compute service that allows you to run code without managing servers.

Answer: B

Explanation: To enable versioning for an Amazon S3 bucket, you need to enable the "Versioning" option for the bucket. This allows you to keep multiple versions of objects in the bucket, providing data durability and recovery options.

Answer: C

Explanation: Amazon Elastic Container Registry (Amazon ECR) is used to manage and store container images for services like Amazon ECS. It allows you to store, manage, and deploy Docker container images in a secure and scalable way.

Answer: A

Explanation: AWS CloudFormation is used to automate the provisioning and management of infrastructure using code. It allows you to define and deploy AWS resources as code, making it easier to manage infrastructure changes.

Answer: B

Explanation: In AWS Elastic Beanstalk, an environment URL provides a public web address for accessing the application deployed in that environment. It allows users and clients to access the application over the internet.

3. Security

Question

1. Imagine that your organization has multiple AWS accounts to isolate a development environment from a production environment. Users in the development account might occasionally need to access resources in the production account. What is the most efficient way to promote an update from the development environment to the production environment?

(A). Create separate identities (and passwords) for users who work in both accounts
(B). Enable Service control policies (SCPs) as a type of organization policy

(C). Grant the users cross-account access
(D). Enable a virtual MFA device for an IAM user

2. Many companies that distribute content over the internet want to restrict access to documents, business data, media streams, or content that is intended for selected users, such as users who have paid a fee. What they can do to securely serve this private content over the internet?
(A). Provide the users access to your private content by using special CloudFront signed URLs or signed cookies
(B). Create a special CloudFront user called an origin access identity and associate it with your Amazon S3
(C). Add trusted signers to an RTMP distribution
(D). Reformat the CloudFront private key

3. Which of the following lifecycle event hooks runs last in an Amazon ECS deployment?
(A).AfterInstall
(B). AfterAllowTraffic
(C) AfterAllowTestTraffic
(D) BeforeInstall

4. You are developing an application that uses Amazon S3. During development, you use your testing-only AWS account to create a bucket named my-data-test, and configures

your application to make requests to my-data-test. You are deploying your application, but you forget to reconfigure the application to use a bucket in your production AWS account. In production, your application makes requests to my-data-test, which succeeds. This results in production data being written to the bucket in your test account. Which of the following features should you use in order to prevent this scenario from happening again?

(A) Enable AWS Config

(B)Use Amazon Macie with Amazon S3

(C)Bucket owner condition

(D)Enable Amazon S3 server access logging

5. You are building an application that will be hosted in ECS which needs to be configured to run its tasks and services using the Fargate launch type. The application will have four different tasks where each task will access various AWS resources that are different from the other tasks. Which of the following solutions can provide your application in ECS access to the required AWS resources?

(A)Create 4 different Service-Linked Roles with the required permissions and attach them to each of the 4 ECS tasks

(B)Create 4 different IAM Roles with the required permissions and attach them to each of the 4 ECS tasks

(C)Create 4 different Container Instance IAM Roles with the required permissions and attach them to each of the 4 ECS tasks

(D) Create an IAM Group with all the required permissions and attach it to each of the 4 ECS tasks

6. You are building the cloud architecture of an application that will be hosted in an EC2 instance. The application will process the data and it will upload the results to an S3 bucket. Which of the following is the best approach to implement this architecture?

(A) Use an IAM Role to grant the application the necessary permissions to upload data to S3

(B) Storing the access keys in the instance and then using the AWS SDK to upload the results to S3

(C) Installing the AWS CLI then using it to upload the results to S3

(D) Using an IAM Inline Policy to grant the application the necessary permissions to upload data to S3

7. You use the AWS Key Management Service (KMS) to create and manage encryption keys across a wide range of AWS services and add an extra layer of security in your application. Which of the following types of Customer master keys (CMKs) would you choose to have full control over these CMKs, including establishing and maintaining their key policies?

(A) AWS managed CMKs

(B)AWS owned CMKs

(C)Customer managed CMKs

(D)Full managed CMKs

You are preparing the CodeDeploy application specification (AppSpec) that uses AWS Lambda compute platform. In the deployment, you need to configure CodeDeploy to run a task after the traffic is shifted to the deployed Lambda function version. Which deployment lifecycle will you configure in this scenario?

(A)

AfterAllowTraffic

(B)

AfterInstall

(C)

AfterAllowTestTraffic

(D)

AllowTraffic

Question 29.

In which of the following scenarios you DON'T need to contact your administrator to help you diagnose and fix common issues that you might encounter when working with Systems Manager and IAM?

(A)

If the AWS Management Console tells you that you're not authorized to perform an action

(B)

If you receive an error that you're not authorized to perform the iam:PassRole action

(C)

fter you create your IAM user access keys and lose your secret key

(D)

To allow others to access Systems Manager, you must create an IAM entity (user or role) for the person or application that needs access

One of the most important things you can do as a customer to ensure the security of your resources is to maintain careful control over who has access to them. This is especially true if any of your AWS users have programmatic access. Programmatic access allows you to invoke actions on your AWS resources either through an application that you write or through a third-party tool. Which of the following actions are considered best practices to help you protect your account and prevent accidental or malicious account activity? (Choose all that apply.)

(A)

Generate access keys for your root account

(B)

Create identities and allow users to log in using a username and password managed by the IAM service

(C)

Grant least privileges to service accounts

(D)

Use AWS Security Token Service to request permanent credentials for use in your code, CLI, or third-party tools

(E)

Utilize Access Advisor

You want to add multi-factor authentication (MFA) to increase the security of your app by adding another authentication method, and not relying solely on user name and password. Which of the following step is a prerequisite before starting the configuration?

(A)

Phone numbers must be verified if MFA is enabled and SMS text message is chosen as a second factor

(B)

Set multi-factor authentication (MFA) to Optional

(C)

Set up and configure a user pool

(D)

Configure and verify an email address or domain to use with your notification emails

By default, Amazon S3 encrypts your data at the object level as it writes it to disks in its data centers and decrypts it when someone accesses it as long as the request is authenticated. Now, you need to add an extra layer of audit trail that shows when your Customer Master Keys (CMK) was used and by whom. Which option will you choose to manage the encryption keys?

(A)

Server-Side Encryption with Amazon S3-Managed Keys (SSE-S3)

(B)

Server-Side Encryption with Customer Master Keys (CMKs) Stored in AWS Key Management Service (SSE-KMS)

(C)

Server-Side Encryption with Customer-Provided Keys (SSE-C)

(D)

You can't add an audit trail that shows when your Customer Master Keys (CMK) was used and by whom

Your company is using AWS Organizations to manage its multiple AWS accounts which are being used by its IT, accounting, and HR departments. To avoid security issues, it is of utmost importance to test the impact of service control policies (SCPs) on your IAM policies and resource policies before applying them. Which of the following AWS services can you use to test and troubleshoot IAM and resource-based policies?

(A)

AWS Control Tower

(B)

AWS Well-Architected Tool

(C)

IAM Policy Simulator

(D)

AWS Organizations

Your organization already uses an identity provider software package such as Microsoft Active Directory that supports SAML 2.0 (Security Assertion Markup Language 2.0). Which of the following solution will you implement if the users that have identities in Microsoft Active Directory need to work with AWS resources?

(A)

Create trust between your organization as an identity provider (IdP) and AWS as the service provide.

(B)

Build a custom identity broker application.

(C)

Use the AWS Mobile SDK for iOS and the AWS Mobile SDK for Android and Fire OS to create unique identities for users.

(D)

Use Amazon Cognito

You are using a Lambda authorizer (formerly known as a custom authorizer) to control access to your API. You need to implement a custom authorization scheme that uses a bearer token authentication strategy such as OAuth to determine the caller's identity. Which of the following methods should you implement the meet requirement?

(A)

Request parameter-based

(B)

IAM permissions

(C)

Cognito Identity Pools

(D)

Token-based

AAWS Systems Manager Parameter Store provides secure, hierarchical storage for configuration data management and secrets management. Which of the following Parameter Store features can benefit your organization? (Choose all that apply.)

(A)

Store configuration data and encrypted strings in hierarchies and track versions

(B)

Improve your security posture by separating your data from your code

(C)

You can use a secure, scalable, hosted secrets management service by managing only one server

(D)

Control and audit access at granular levels

(E)

Improve your security posture by keeping your data from your code in the same place

For compliance purposes, you need to assess how well your resource configurations comply with internal practices, industry guidelines, and regulations. Which of the following tools will you use to meet the requirement?

(A)

AWS Security Hub.

(B)

AWS Config

(C)

AWS Shield

(D)

AWS Health

You are working on a project that uses Microsft SQL Server 2019 Standard Edition for a database. To add an extra layer of security you need to configure the DB to encrypts data before it is written to storage, and automatically decrypts data when the data is read from storage. Which of the following actions will you follow to achieve this?

(A)

Enable Transparent Data Encryption (TDE)

(B)

Enable Kerberos authentication

(C)

IAM database authentication

(D)

Use DynamoDB Encryption Client

Which of the following is the practice of encrypting plaintext data with a data key, and then encrypting the data key under another key?

(A)

Encryption context

(B)

Envelope encryption

(C)

Key policies

(D)

Key usage

Which of the following AWS Services enables you to replace hardcoded credentials in your code, with an API call that retrieves the secret programmatically to ensure that the secret can't be compromised by someone examining your code?

(A)

AWS Security Hub

(B)

AWS Secrets Manager

(C)

AWS Shield Advanced

(D)

AWS Resource Groups

Answers

Imagine that your organization has multiple AWS accounts to isolate a development environment from a production environment. Users in the development account might occasionally need to access resources in the production account. What is the most efficient way to promote an update from the development environment to the production environment?

(A) Create separate identities (and passwords) for users who work in both accounts

(B) Enable Service control policies (SCPs) as a type of organization policy

(C)Grant the users cross-account access

(D) Enable a virtual MFA device for an IAM user

Explanations

Grant the users cross-account access is the correct answer.

Using IAM roles, you can take advantage of cross-account access to give users access across AWS accounts when they need it.

Create separate identities (and passwords) for users who work in both accounts is incorrect.

This answer is technically correct but we need to find the most efficient way to promote an update from the development environment to the production environment. Managing credentials for multiple accounts makes identity management difficult.

Enable Service control policies (SCPs) as a type of organization policy is incorrect.

Service control policies (SCPs) are a type of organization policy that you can use to manage permissions in your organization. SCPs offer central control over the maximum available permissions for all accounts in your organization. SCPs help you to ensure your accounts stay within your organization's access control guidelines.

Enable a virtual MFA device for an IAM user is incorrect
becaue enabling MFA increase the overall security of the system, it can't promote any update from the development environment to the production environment.

Many companies that distribute content over the internet want to restrict access to documents, business data, media streams, or content that is intended for selected users, such as users who have paid a fee. What they can do to securely serve this private content over the internet?

(A) Provide the users access to your private content by using special CloudFront signed URLs or signed cookies

(B)

Create a special CloudFront user called an origin access identity and associate it with your Amazon S3

(C)

Add trusted signers to an RTMP distribution

(D)

Reformat the CloudFront private key

Provide the users access to your private content by using special CloudFront signed URLs or signed cookies is the correct answer

•

Many companies that distribute content over the internet want to restrict access to documents, business data, media streams, or content that is intended for selected users, for example, users who have paid a fee.

To securely serve this private content by using CloudFront, you can do the following:

1. Require that your users access your private content by using special CloudFront signed URLs or signed cookies.

2. Require that your users access your content by using CloudFront URLs, not URLs that access content directly on the origin server (for example, Amazon S3 or a private HTTP server). Requiring CloudFront URLs isn't necessary, but we recommend it to prevent users from bypassing the restrictions that you specify in signed URLs or signed

cookies.

Create a special CloudFront user called an origin access identity and associate it with your Amazon S3 is incorrect because you can create a special CloudFront user and associate that user with the Amazon S3, this user can be associated ONLY with the CloudFront distribution.

Add trusted signers to an RTMP distribution is incorrect
because the content from the companies is distributed using the Internet Protocol (IP) not the Real-Time Messaging Protocol (RTMP).

Reformat the CloudFront private key is incorrect
as this option could be used if you were using .NET or Java to create signed URLs or signed cookies.

Which of the following lifecycle event hooks runs last in an Amazon ECS deployment?

(A) AfterInstall

(B) AfterAllowTraffic

(C) AfterAllowTestTraffic

(D)

BeforeInstall

Explanation 23. AfterAllowTraffic is the correct answer.
In an Amazon ECS deployment, event hooks run in the following order:

Note:
The
Start, Install, TestTraffic, AllowTraffic,
and

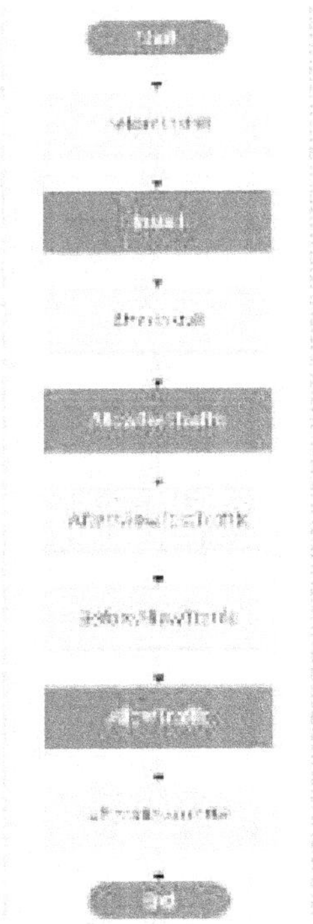

End

events in the deployment cannot be scripted, which is why they appear in gray in this diagram .

BeforeInstall

– Use to run tasks before the replacement task set is created. One target group is associated with the original task set. If an optional test listener is specified, it is associated with the original task set. A rollback is not possible at this point.

AfterInstall

– Use to run tasks after the replacement task set is created and one of the target groups is associated with it. If an optional test listener is specified, it is associated with the original task set. The results of a hook function at this lifecycle event can trigger a rollback.

AfterAllowTestTraffic

– Use to run tasks after the test listener serves traffic to the replacement task set. The results of a hook function at this point can trigger a rollback.

BeforeAllowTraffic

– Use to run tasks after the second target group is associated with the replacement task set, but before traffic is shifted to the replacement task set. The results of a hook functiontion at this lifecycle event can trigger a rollback.

AfterAllowTraffic – Use to run tasks after the second target group serves traffic to the replacement task set. The results of a hook function at this lifecycle event can trigger a rollback.

You are developing an application that uses Amazon S3. During development, you use your testing-only AWS account to create a bucket named my-data-test, and configures your application to make requests to my-data-test. You are deploying your application, but you forget to reconfigure the application to use a bucket in your production AWS account. In production, your application makes requests to my-data-test, which succeeds. This results in production data being written to the bucket in your test account. Which of the following features should you use in order to prevent this scenario from happening again?

(A) Enable AWS Config

(B)Use Amazon Macie with Amazon S3

(C)Bucket owner condition

(D)Enable Amazon S3 server access logging

Bucket owner condition is the correct answer.

We recommend using bucket owner condition whenever you perform a supported S3 operation and know the account ID of the expected bucket owner.

With bucket owner condition, you can include the AWS account ID of the expected bucket owner in your requests. Amazon S3 then checks the account ID of the bucket owner before processing each request. If the actual bucket owner doesn't match the expected bucket owner, the request fails.

If you use bucket owner condition, the scenario described earlier won't result in your application inadvertently writing to a test bucket. Instead, the requests that your application makes will fail with a descriptive error message. By using bucket owner condition, you help eliminate the risk of accidentally interacting with buckets in the wrong

AWS account.

Enable AWS Config is incorrect.
AWS Config enables you to assess, audit, and evaluate the configurations of your AWS resources. AWS Config monitors resource configurations, allowing you to evaluate the recorded configurations against the desired secure configurations.

Use Amazon Macie with Amazon S3 is incorrect.
Macie uses machine learning to automatically discover, classify, and protect sensitive data in AWS. Macie recognizes sensitive data such as personally identifiable information (PII) or intellectual property. It provides you with dashboards and alerts that give visibility into how this data is being accessed or moved.

Enable Amazon S3 server access logging is incorrect. Server access logging provides detailed records of the requests that are made to a bucket. Server access logs can assist you in security and access audits, help you learn about your customer base, and understand your Amazon S3 bill.

You are building an application that will be hosted in ECS which needs to be configured to run its tasks and services using the Fargate launch type. The application will have four different tasks where each task will access various AWS resources that are different from the other tasks. Which of the following solutions can provide your application in ECS access to the required AWS resources?

(A)

Create 4 different Service-Linked Roles with the required permissions and attach them to each of the 4 ECS tasks

(B) Create 4 different IAM Roles with the required permissions and attach them to each of the 4 ECS tasks

(C)

Create 4 different Container Instance IAM Roles with the required permissions and attach them to each of the 4 ECS tasks

(D)

Create an IAM Group with all the required permissions and attach it to each of the 4

ECS tasks

Create 4 different IAM Roles with the required permissions and attach them to each of the 4 ECS tasks is the correct answer.

By default, IAM users don't have permission to create or modify Amazon ECS resources, or perform tasks using the Amazon ECS API. This means that they also can't do so using the Amazon ECS console or the AWS CLI. To allow IAM users to create or modify resources and perform tasks, you must create IAM policies. Policies grant IAM users permissions to use specific resources and API actions. Then, attach those policies to the IAM users or groups that require those permissions.

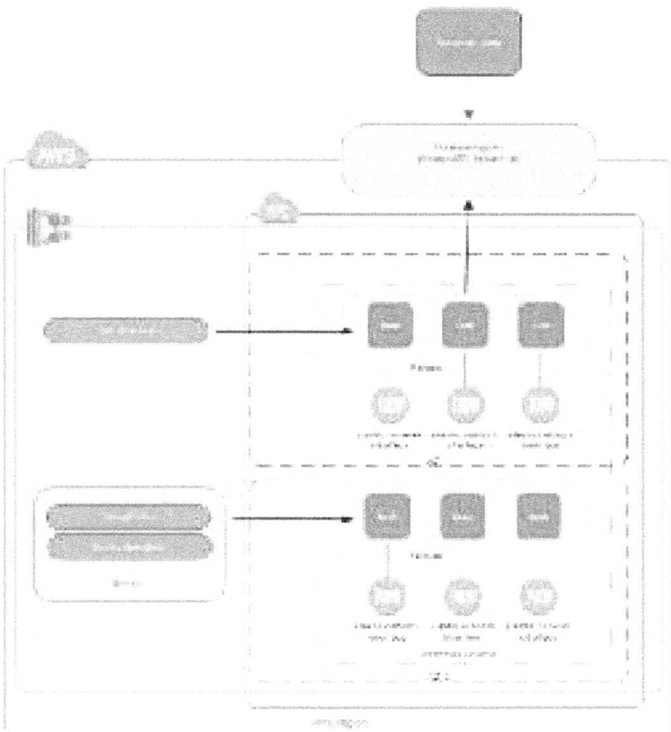

When you attach a policy to a user or group of users, it allows or denies the users permission to perform the specified tasks on the specified resources. Likewise, Amazon ECS container instances make calls to the Amazon ECS and Amazon EC2 APIs on your behalf, so they need to authenticate with your credentials. This authentication is accomplished by creating an IAM role for your container instances and associating that role with your container instances when you launch them.

If you use an Elastic Load Balancing load balancer with your Amazon ECS services, calls to the Amazon EC2 and Elastic Load Balancing APIs are made on your behalf to register and deregister container instances with your load balancers.

Hence, the correct answer is create 4 different IAM Roles with the required permissions and attach it to each of the 4 ECS tasks.

Creating an IAM Group with all the required permissions and attaching them to each of the 4 ECS tasks is incorrect
because you cannot directly attach an IAM Group to an ECS Task. Attaching an IAM Role is a more suitable solution in this scenario and not an IAM Group.

Creating 4 different Container Instance IAM Roles with the required permissions and attaching them to each of the 4 ECS tasks is incorrect
because a Container Instance IAM Role only applies if you are using the EC2 launch type. Take note that the scenario says that the application will be using a Fargate launch type.

Creating 4 different Service-Linked Roles with the required permissions and attaching them to each of the 4 ECS tasks is incorrect
because a service-linked role is a unique type of IAM role that is linked directly to Amazon ECS itself and not on the ECS task. Service-linked roles are predefined by Amazon ECS and include all the permissions that the service requires to call other AWS services on your behalf.

You are building the cloud architecture of an application that will be hosted in an EC2 instance. The application will process the data and it will upload the results to an S3 bucket. Which of the following is the best approach to implement this architecture?

(A) Use an IAM Role to grant the application the necessary permissions to upload data to S3

(B) Storing the access keys in the instance and then using the AWS SDK to upload the

results to S3
(C) Installing the AWS CLI then using it to upload the results to S3
(D) Using an IAM Inline Policy to grant the application the necessary permissions to upload data to S3

Use an IAM Role to grant the application the necessary permissions to upload data to S3 is the correct answer.
Applications that run on an EC2 instance must include AWS credentials in their AWS API requests. You could have your developers store AWS credentials directly within the EC2 instance and allow applications in that instance to use those credentials. But developers would then have to manage the credentials and ensure that they securely pass the credentials to each instance and update each EC2 instance when it's time to rotate the credentials. That's a lot of additional work.

Instead, you can and should use an IAM role to manage temporary credentials for applications that run on an EC2 instance. When you use a role, you don't have to distribute long-term credentials (such as a user name and password or access keys) to an EC2 instance. Instead, the role supplies temporary permissions that applications can use when they make calls to other AWS resources.

When you launch an EC2 instance, you specify an IAM role to associate with the instance. Applications that run on the instance can then use the role-supplied temporary credentials to sign API requests. In the following figure, a developer runs an application on an EC2 instance that requires access to the S3 bucket named photos. An administrator creates the Get-pics . service role and attaches the role to the EC2 instance.

The role includes a permissions policy that grants read-only access to the specified S3 bucket. It also includes a trust policy that allows the EC2 instance to assume the role and retrieve the temporary credentials. When the application runs on the instance, it can use the role's temporary credentials to access the photos bucket. The administrator doesn't have to grant the developer permission to access the photos bucket, and the developer never has to share or manage credentials.

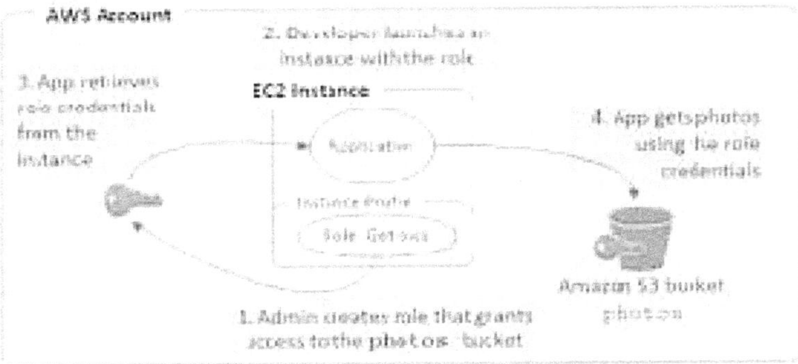

Storing the access keys in the instance and then using the AWS SDK to upload the results to S3
is incorrect because this will expose the AWS access credentials to all users who have access to the EC2 instance. Since this option entails a security risk, this is incorrect as is not the safest method.

Installing the AWS CLI then using it to upload the results to S3 is incorrect
because although this option is valid, this method also presents a security risk just as shown above. By default, an AWS CLI requires you to store the AWS access keys in your instance which will be used in executing the commands.

Using an IAM Inline Policy to grant the application the necessary permissions to upload data to S3 is incorrect
because inline policies are useful if you want to maintain a strict one-to-one relationship between a policy and the principal entity that it's applied to. This option doesn't provide a secure way of allowing the application that is hosted in EC2 to upload data to an S3 bucket. You should use an IAM Role instead.

You use the AWS Key Management Service (KMS) to create and manage encryption keys across a wide range of AWS services and add an extra layer of security in your application. Which of the following types of Customer master keys (CMKs) would you choose to have full control over these CMKs, including establishing and maintaining their key policies?

(A) AWS managed CMKs
(B)AWS owned CMKs
(C)Customer managed CMKs
(D)Full managed CMKs

Explanation. Customer managed CMKs is the correct answer.

A customer master key (CMK) is a logical representation of a master key. The CMK includes metadata, such as the key ID, creation date, description, and key state. The CMK also contains the key material used to encrypt and decrypt data.

AWS KMS supports symmetric and asymmetric CMKs. A symmetric CMK represents a 256-bit key that is used for encryption and decryption. An asymmetric CMK represents an RSA key pair that is used for encryption and decryption or signing and verification (but not both), or an elliptic curve (ECC) key pair that is used for signing and verification.

AWS KMS supports three types of CMKs: customer managed CMKs, AWS managed CMKs, and AWS owned CMKs.

Customer managed CMKs are CMKs in your AWS account that you create, own, and manage. You have full control over these CMKs, including establishing and maintaining their key policies, IAM policies, and grants, enabling and disabling them, rotating their cryptographic material, adding tags, creating aliases that refer to the CMK, and scheduling the CMKs for deletion.

AWS managed CMKs is incorrect.
AWS managed CMKs are CMKs in your account that are created, managed, and used on your behalf by an AWS service that is integrated with AWS KMS.

AWS owned CMKs is incorrect.
AWS owned CMKs are a collection of CMKs that an AWS service owns and manages for use in multiple AWS accounts. Although AWS owned CMKs are not in your AWS ac-

count, an AWS service can use its AWS owned CMKs to protect the resources in your account.

Full managed CMKs is incorrect as there is no such type of Customer master keys (CMKs).

You are preparing the CodeDeploy application specification (AppSpec) that uses AWS Lambda compute platform. In the deployment, you need to configure CodeDeploy to run a task after the traffic is shifted to the deployed Lambda function version. Which deployment lifecycle will you configure in this scenario?

(A) AfterAllowTraffic

(B)

AfterInstall

(C)

AfterAllowTestTraffic

(D)

AllowTraffic

AfterAllowTraffic is the correct answer.

The content in the 'hooks' section of the AppSpec file varies, depending on the compute platform for your deployment. The 'hooks' section for a Lambda or an Amazon ECS deployment specifies Lambda validation functions to run during a deployment lifecycle event. If an event hook is not present, no operation is executed for that event.

An AWS Lambda hook is one Lambda function specified with a string on a new line after the name of the lifecycle event. Each hook is executed once per deployment. Here are descriptions of the hooks available for use in your AppSpec file.

BeforeAllowTraffic – Use to run tasks before traffic is shifted to the deployed Lambda function version.

AfterAllowTraffic – Use to run tasks after all traffic is shifted to the deployed Lambda function version.

In a serverless Lambda function version deployment, event hooks run in the following order:

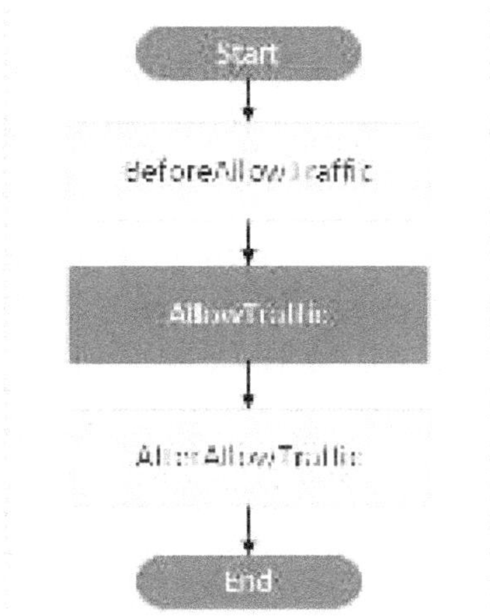

Note:
The Start, AllowTraffic, and End events in the deployment cannot be scripted, which is why they appear in gray in this diagram.

AfterInstall and

AfterAllowTestTraffic are incorrect

because these events are only applicable for ECS, EC2 or On-Premises compute platforms and not for Lambda deployments

AllowTraffic is incorrect

because this deployment lifecycle event in Lambda cannot be scripted or used.

In which of the following scenarios you DON'T need to contact your administrator to help you diagnose and fix common issues that you might encounter when working with Systems Manager and IAM?

(A) If the AWS Management Console tells you that you're not authorized to perform an action

(B) If you receive an error that you're not authorized to perform the iam:PassRole action

(C) After you create your IAM user access keys and lose your secret key

(D) To allow others to access Systems Manager, you must create an IAM entity (user or role) for the person or application that needs access

Explanation. After you create your IAM user access keys and lose your secret key is the correct answer.

After you create your IAM user access keys, you can view your access key ID at any time. However, you can't view your secret access key again. If you lose your secret key, you must create a new access key pair without the need of the administrator.

If the AWS Management Console tells you that you're not authorized to perform an action is incorrect.

If the AWS Management Console tells you that you're not authorized to perform an action, then you must contact your administrator for assistance. Your administrator is the person that provided you with your user name and password.

The following example error occurs when the Examsdigest-user2 IAM user tries to use the console to view details about a document but does not have ssm:GetDocument permissions.

User: arn:aws:ssm::123456789012:user/examsdigest-user2 is not authorized to perform: ssm:GetDocument on resource: MyExampleDocument

In this case, Examsdigest-user2 asks his administrator to update his policies to allow him to access the MyExampleDocument resource using the ssm:GetDocument action.

If you receive an error that you're not authorized to perform the iam:PassRole action is incorrect.

If you receive an error that you're not authorized to perform the iam:PassRole action, then you must contact your administrator for assistance. Your administrator is the person that provided you with your user name and password. Ask that person to update your policies to allow you to pass a role to Systems Manager.

To allow others to access Systems Manager, you must create an IAM entity (user or role) for the person or application that needs access is incorrect.

To allow others to access Systems Manager, administrators must create an IAM entity (user or role) for the person or application that needs access. They will use the credentials for that entity to access AWS. Administrators then attach a policy to the entity that grants them the correct permissions in Systems Manager.

One of the most important things you can do as a customer to ensure the security of your resources is to maintain careful control over who has access to them. This is especially true if any of your AWS users have programmatic access. Programmatic access allows you to invoke actions on your AWS resources either through an application that you write or through a third-party tool. Which of the following actions are considered best practices to help you protect your account and prevent accidental or malicious account activity? (Choose all that apply.)

(A) Generate access keys for your root account

(B) Create identities and allow users to log in using a username and password managed by the IAM service

(C) Grant least privileges to service accounts

(D) Use AWS Security Token Service to request permanent credentials for use in your code, CLI, or third-party tools

(E) Utilize Access Advisor

Explanation. The correct answers are:

1. Create identities and allow users to log in using a username and password managed by the IAM service

2. Grant least privileges to service accounts

3. Utilize Access Advisor

I'll highlight some general guidelines to help you protect your account, as well as some of the options you have when you need to provide programmatic access to your AWS resources.

1. Protect your root account

Your AWS root account—the account that's created when you initially sign up with AWS—has unrestricted access to all your AWS resources. There's no way to limit permissions on a root account. For this reason,

AWS always recommends that you DO NOT generate access keys for your root account.

2. Decide how to grant access to your AWS account

To allow users access to the AWS Management Console and AWS Command Line Interface (AWS CLI), you have two options. The first one is to create identities and allow users to log in using a username and password managed by the IAM service. The second approach is to use federation.

3. Grant least privileges to service accounts
If you decided to create service accounts (that is, accounts used for programmatic access by applications running outside of the AWS environment) and generate access keys for them, you should create a dedicated service account for each use case.

4. Use temporary credentials from AWS STS
AWS Security Token Service (AWS STS) is a web service that enables you to request TEMPORARY credentials for use in your code, CLI, or third-party tools. It allows you to assume an IAM role with which you have a trusted relationship and then generate temporary, time-limited credentials based on the permissions associated with the role.

5. Utilize Access Advisor
The IAM console provides information about when an AWS service was last accessed by different principals. This information is called service last accessed data.

Using this tool, you can view when an IAM user, group, role, or policy last attempted to access services to which they have permissions. Based on this information, you can decide if certain permissions need to be revoked or restricted further.

You want to add multi-factor authentication (MFA) to increase the security of your app by adding another authentication method, and not relying solely on user name and password. Which of the following step is a prerequisite before starting the configuration?

(A) Phone numbers must be verified if MFA is enabled and SMS text message is chosen as a second factor

(B) Set multi-factor authentication (MFA) to Optional

(C) Set up and configure a user pool

(D) Configure and verify an email address or domain to use with your notification emails

Explanation. Phone numbers must be verified if MFA is enabled and SMS text message is chosen as a second factor is the correct answer.

Multi-factor authentication (MFA) increases security for your app by adding another authentication method, and not relying solely on user name and password. You can choose to use SMS text messages, or time-based one-time (TOTP) passwords as second factors in signing in your users.

Prerequisites

Before you begin, you need:

You can only choose MFA as

Required

when you initially create a user pool.

Phone numbers must be verified if MFA is enabled and

SMS text message

is chosen as a second factor.

Advanced security features require that MFA is enabled, and set as optional in the Amazon Cognito user pool console.

By default, Amazon S3 encrypts your data at the object level as it writes it to disks in its data centers and decrypts it when someone accesses it as long as the request is authenticated. Now, you need to add an extra layer of audit trail that shows when your Customer Master Keys (CMK) was used and by whom. Which option will you choose to manage the encryption keys?

(A) Server-Side Encryption with Amazon S3-Managed Keys (SSE-S3)

(B) Server-Side Encryption with Customer Master Keys (CMKs) Stored in AWS Key Management Service (SSE-KMS)

(C) Server-Side Encryption with Customer-Provided Keys (SSE-C)

(D) You can't add an audit trail that shows when your Customer Master Keys (CMK) was used and by whom

Explanation

Server-Side Encryption with Customer Master Keys (CMKs) Stored in AWS Key Management Service (SSE-KMS) is the correct answer.

Server-Side Encryption with Customer Master Keys (CMKs) Stored in AWS Key Management Service (SSE-KMS) is similar to SSE-S3, but with some additional benefits and charges for using this service.

There are separate permissions for the use of a CMK that provides added protection against unauthorized access of your objects in Amazon S3. SSE-KMS also provides you with an audit trail that shows when your CMK was used and by whom. Additionally, you can create and manage customer-managed CMKs or use AWS managed CMKs that are unique to you, your service, and your Region.

Server-Side Encryption with Amazon S3-Managed Keys (SSE-S3) is incorrect.

When you use Server-Side Encryption with Amazon S3-Managed Keys (SSE-S3), each object is encrypted with a unique key. As an additional safeguard, it encrypts the key itself with a master key that it regularly rotates. Amazon S3 server-side encryption uses one of the strongest block ciphers available, 256-bit Advanced Encryption Standard (AES-256), to encrypt your data.

Server-Side Encryption with Customer-Provided Keys (SSE-C) is incorrect.

With Server-Side Encryption with Customer-Provided Keys (SSE-C), you manage the encryption keys and Amazon S3 manages the encryption, as it writes to disks, and decryption when you access your objects.

You can't add an audit trail that shows when your Customer Master Keys (CMK) was used and by whom is incorrect

because we can use Server-Side Encryption with Customer Master Keys (CMKs) Stored in AWS Key

Question

Your company is using AWS Organizations to manage its multiple AWS accounts which are being used by its IT, accounting, and HR departments. To avoid security issues, it is of utmost importance to test the impact of service control policies (SCPs) on your IAM policies and resource policies before applying them. Which of the following AWS services can you use to test and troubleshoot IAM and resource-based policies?

(A) AWS Control Tower

(B) AWS Well-Architected Tool

(C) IAM Policy Simulator

(D) AWS Organizations

Explanation. IAM Policy Simulator is the correct answer.

With the IAM policy simulator, you can test and troubleshoot identity-based policies, IAM permissions boundaries, Organizations service control policies (SCPs), and resource-based policies.

Here are some common things you can do with the policy simulator:

1. Test policies that are attached to IAM users, groups, or roles in your AWS account. If more than one policy is attached to the user, group, or role, you can test all the policies, or select individual policies to test. You can test which actions are allowed or denied by the selected policies for specific resources.

2. Test and troubleshoot the effect of permissions boundaries on IAM entities. Note: you can only simulate one permissions boundary at a time.

3. Test policies that are attached to AWS resources, such as Amazon S3 buckets, Amazon SQS queues, Amazon SNS topics, or Amazon S3 Glacier vaults.

4. If your AWS account is a member of an organization in AWS Organizations, then you can test the impact of service control policies (SCPs) on your IAM policies and resource policies.

5. Test new policies that are not yet attached to a user, group, or role by typing or copying them into the simulator. These are used only in the simulation and are not saved.

6. Test the policies with selected services, actions, and resources. For example, you can test to ensure that your policy allows an entity to perform the ListAllMyBuckets, Create-Bucket, and DeleteBucket actions in the Amazon S3 service on a specific bucket.

7. Simulate real-world scenarios by providing context keys, such as an IP address or date, that are included in Condition elements in the policies being tested.

8. Identify which specific statement in policy results in allowing or denying access to a particular resource or action.

AWS Control Tower is incorrect.
AWS Control Tower is a service that enables you to enforce and manage governance rules for security, operations, and compliance at scale across all your organizations and accounts in the AWS Cloud.

AWS Well-Architected Tool is incorrect.
Use the AWS Well-Architected Tool to review your workloads against current AWS architectural best practices. The AWS Well-Architected Tool measures the workload and provides recommendations on how to improve your architecture.

AWS Organizations is incorrect.
AWS Organizations is an account management service that lets you consolidate multiple AWS accounts into an organization that you create and centrally manage. With AWS Organizations, you can create member accounts and invite existing accounts to join your organization. You can organize those accounts and manage them as a group.

Question
Your organization already uses an identity provider software package such as Microsoft Active Directory that supports SAML 2.0 (Security Assertion Markup Language 2.0). Which of the following solution will you implement if the users that have identities in Microsoft Active Directory need to work with AWS resources?
(A) Create trust between your organization as an identity provider (IdP) and AWS as the service provide

(B) Build a custom identity broker application

(C) Use the AWS Mobile SDK for iOS and the AWS Mobile SDK for Android and Fire OS to create unique identities for users

(D) Use Amazon Cognito

Explanation

Create trust between your organization as an identity provider (IdP) and AWS as the service provider is the correct answer.

If your organization already uses an identity provider software package that supports SAML 2.0 (Security Assertion Markup Language 2.0), you can create trust between your organization as an identity provider (IdP) and AWS as the service provider.

You can then use SAML to provide your users with federated single-sign on (SSO) to the AWS Management Console or federated access to call AWS API operations. For example, if your company uses Microsoft Active Directory and Active Directory Federation Services, then you can federate using SAML 2.0.

Build a custom identity broker application is incorrect
because the identity store is compatible with SAML 2.0. You can build a custom identity broker application when the identity store is NOT compatible with SAML 2.0.

Use the AWS Mobile SDK for iOS and the AWS Mobile SDK for Android and Fire OS to create unique identities for users is incorrect
because these can be used if you create a mobile or web-based app that accesses AWS resources.

Use Amazon Cognito is incorrect because this is used for mobile and web-based application scenarios.

Question

You are using a Lambda authorizer (formerly known as a custom authorizer) to control access to your API. You need to implement a custom authorization scheme that uses a bearer token authentication strategy such as OAuth to determine the caller's identity. Which of the following methods should you implement the meet requirement?

(A) Request parameter-based

(B)IAM permissions

(C)Cognito Identity Pools

(D) Token-based

Explanation Token-based is the correct answer.

A Lambda authorizer (formerly known as a *custom authorizer)* is an API Gateway feature that uses a Lambda function to control access to your API.

A Lambda authorizer is useful if you want to implement a custom authorization scheme that uses a bearer token authentication strategy such as OAuth or SAML, or that uses request parameters to determine the caller's identity.

When a client makes a request to one of your API's methods, API Gateway calls your Lambda authorizer, which takes the caller's identity as input and returns an IAM policy as output.

There are two types of Lambda authorizers:
A token-based Lambda authorizer (also called a TOKEN authorizer) receives the caller's identity in a bearer token, such as a JSON Web Token (JWT) or an OAuth token.

A request parameter-based Lambda authorizer (also called a REQUEST authorizer) receives the caller's identity in a combination of headers, query string parameters, stage-Variables, and $context variables.

Request parameter-based is incorrect.
Request parameter-based receives the caller's identity in a combination of headers,

query string parameters, stageVariables, and $context variables.

IAM permissions is incorrect.
IAM permissions is technically correct as it controls access to your Amazon API Gateway but in our case, we need to receive the caller's identity in a bearer token.

Amazon Cognito identity pools is incorrect.
Amazon Cognito identity pools (federated identities) enable you to create unique identities for your users and federate them with identity providers. With an identity pool, you can obtain temporary, limited-privilege AWS credentials to access other AWS services.

Question

AWS Systems Manager Parameter Store provides secure, hierarchical storage for configuration data management and secrets management. Which of the following Parameter Store features can benefit your organization? (Choose all that apply.)

(A) Store configuration data and encrypted strings in hierarchies and track versions

(B) Improve your security posture by separating your data from your code

(C) You can use a secure, scalable, hosted secrets management service by managing only one server

(D) Control and audit access at granular levels

(E) Improve your security posture by keeping your data from your code in the same place

Explanation . The correct answers are:

1. Store configuration data and encrypted strings in hierarchies and track versions

2. Improve your security posture by separating your data from your code

3. Control and audit access at granular levels

AWS Systems Manager Parameter Store provides secure, hierarchical storage for configuration data management and secrets management. You can store data such as passwords, database strings, Amazon Machine Image (AMI) IDs, and license codes as parameter values. You can store values as plain text or encrypted data. You can reference Systems Manager parameters in your scripts, commands, SSM documents, and configuration and automation workflows by using the unique name that you specified when you created the parameter.

How can Parameter Store benefit my organization?
Parameter Store offers these benefits:
- You can use a secure, scalable, hosted secrets management service with no servers to manage.
- Improve your security posture by separating your data from your code.
- Store configuration data and encrypted strings in hierarchies and track versions.
-Control and audit access at granular levels.

Who should use Parameter Store?
-Any AWS customer who wants to have a centralized way to manage configuration data.

- Software developers who want to easily store different logins and reference streams.

- Administrators who want to be notified when changes have or have not been made to secrets and passwords.

Question
For compliance purposes, you need to assess how well your resource configurations comply with internal practices, industry guidelines, and regulations. Which of the following tools will you use to meet the requirement?

(A) AWS Security Hub.
(B) AWS Config
(C) AWS Shield

(D) AWS Health

Explanation. AWS Config is the correct answer.

AWS Config can be used to assess how well your resource configurations comply with internal practices, industry guidelines, and regulations.

AWS Security Hub is correct.
AWS Security Hub provides you with a comprehensive view of your security state in AWS and helps you check your environment against security industry standards and best practices.

Security Hub collects security data from across AWS accounts, services, and supported third-party partner products and helps you analyze your security trends and identify the highest priority security issues

AWS Shield is incorrect.
AWS provides two levels of protection against DDoS attacks: AWS Shield Standard and AWS Shield Advanced. AWS Shield Standard is automatically included at no extra cost beyond what you already pay for AWS WAF and your other AWS services.

For added protection against DDoS attacks, AWS offers AWS Shield Advanced. AWS Shield Advanced provides expanded DDoS attack protection for your Amazon EC2 instances, Elastic Load Balancing load balancers, Amazon CloudFront distributions, and Amazon Route 53 hosted zones.

AWS Health is incorrect.
AWS Health provides personalized information about events that can affect your AWS infrastructure, guides you through scheduled changes, and accelerates the troubleshooting of issues that affect your AWS resources and accounts.

Question
You are working on a project that uses Microsft SQL Server 2019 Standard Edition for a

database. To add an extra layer of security you need to configure the DB to encrypts data before it is written to storage, and automatically decrypts data when the data is read from storage. Which of the following actions will you follow to achieve this?

(A) Enable Transparent Data Encryption (TDE)

(B)Enable Kerberos authentication

(C)IAM database authentication

(D)Use DynamoDB Encryption Client

Explanation. Enable Transparent Data Encryption (TDE) is the correct answer.

Amazon RDS supports using Transparent Data Encryption (TDE) to encrypt stored data on your DB instances running Microsoft SQL Server. TDE automatically encrypts data before it is written to storage, and automatically decrypts data when the data is read from storage.

Amazon RDS supports TDE for the following SQL Server versions and editions:

SQL Server 2019 Standard and Enterprise Editions

SQL Server 2017 Enterprise Edition

SQL Server 2016 Enterprise Edition

SQL Server 2014 Enterprise Edition

SQL Server 2012 Enterprise Edition

To enable transparent data encryption for an RDS SQL Server DB instance, specify the TDE option in an RDS option group that is associated with that DB instance.

Enable Kerberos authentication is incorrect

. Kerberos is a network authentication protocol that uses tickets and symmetric-key cryptography to eliminate the need to transmit passwords over the network. Kerberos has been built into Active Directory and is designed to authenticate users to network resources, such as databases.

Amazon RDS support for Kerberos and Active Directory provides the benefits of single sign-on and centralized authentication of database users.

IAM database authentication is incorrect.
You can authenticate to your DB instance using AWS Identity and Access Management (IAM) database authentication. IAM database authentication works with MySQL and PostgreSQL. With this authentication method, you don't need to use a password when you connect to a DB instance. Instead, you use an authentication token.

Use DynamoDB Encryption Client is incorrect.
The Amazon DynamoDB Encryption Client is a software library that helps you to protect your table data before you send it to Amazon DynamoDB. Encrypting your sensitive data in transit and at rest helps ensure that your plaintext data isn't available to any third party, including AWS.

Question
Which of the following is the practice of encrypting plaintext data with a data key, and then encrypting the data key under another key?
(A) Encryption context
(B)Envelope encryption
(C)Key policies
(D)Key usage

Explanation. Envelope encryption is the correct answer.
When you encrypt your data, your data is protected, but you have to protect your encryption key. One strategy is to encrypt it. Envelope encryption is the practice of encrypting plaintext data with a data key, and then encrypting the data key under another key.

You can even encrypt the data encryption key under another encryption key, and encrypt that encryption key under another encryption key. But, eventually, one key must remain in plaintext so you can decrypt the keys and your data. This top-level plaintext key encryption key is known as the master key.

AWS KMS helps you to protect your master keys by storing and managing them securely. Master keys stored in AWS KMS, known as customer master keys (CMKs), never leave the AWS KMS FIPS validated hardware security modules unencrypted. To use an AWS KMS CMK, you must call AWS KMS.

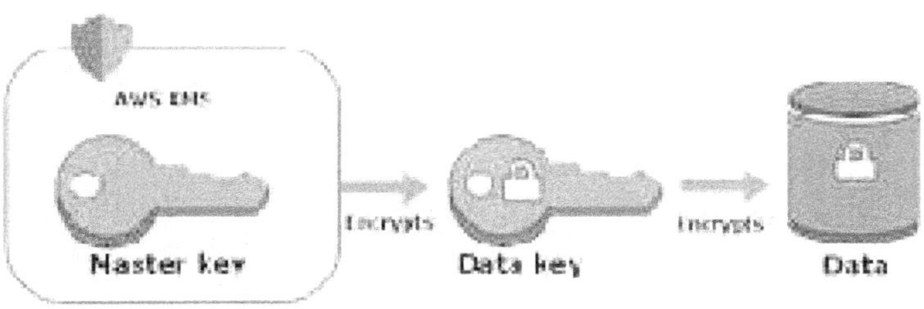

Envelope encryption offers several benefits:

1. Protecting data keys
When you encrypt a data key, you don't have to worry about storing the encrypted data key, because the data key is inherently protected by encryption. You can safely store the encrypted data key alongside the encrypted data.

2. Encrypting the same data under multiple master keys

Encryption operations can be time consuming, particularly when the data being encrypted are large objects. Instead of re-encrypting raw data multiple times with different keys, you can re-encrypt only the data keys that protect the raw data.

3. Combining the strengths of multiple algorithms

In general, symmetric key algorithms are faster and produce smaller ciphertexts than public key algorithms. But public key algorithms provide inherent separation of roles and easier key management. Envelope encryption lets you combine the strengths of each strategy.

Encryption context is incorrect.
All AWS KMS cryptographic operations with symmetric CMKs accept an encryption context, an optional set of key–value pairs that can contain additional contextual information about the data. AWS KMS uses the encryption context as additional authenticated data (AAD) to support authenticated encryption.

Key policies is incorrect.
When you create a CMK, you determine who can use and manage that CMK. These permissions are contained in a document called the key policy. You can use the key policy to add, remove, or change permissions at any time for a customer-managed CMK. But you cannot edit the key policy for an AWS managed CMK.

Key usage is incorrect.
Key usage is a CMK property that determines whether a CMK is used for encryption and decryption -or- signing and verification. You cannot choose both. Using a CMK for more than one type of operation makes the product of both operations more vulnerable to attack.

Question
Which of the following AWS Services enables you to replace hardcoded credentials in your code, with an API call that retrieves the secret programmatically to ensure that the secret can't be compromised by someone examining your code?

(A) AWS Security Hub
(B) AWS Secrets Manager
(C)AWS Shield Advanced
(D) AWS Resource Groups

Explanations

AWS Secrets Manager is the correct answer.
In the past, when you created a custom application to retrieve information from a database, you typically embedded the credentials, the secret, for accessing the database directly in the application. When the time came to rotate the credentials, you had to do more than just create new credentials.

You had to invest time to update the application to use the new credentials. Then you distributed the updated application. If you had multiple applications with shared credentials and you missed updating one of them, the application failed. Because of this risk, many customers choose not to regularly rotate credentials, which effectively substitutes one risk for another.

Secrets Manager enables
you to replace hardcoded credentials in your code, including passwords, with an API call to Secrets Manager to retrieve the secret programmatically. This helps ensure the secret can't be compromised by someone examining your code, because the secret no longer exists in the code. Also, you can configure Secrets Manager to automatically rotate the secret for you according to a specified schedule. This enables you to replace long-term secrets with short-term ones, significantly reducing the risk of compromise.

AWS Security Hub is incorrect.
AWS Security Hub provides you with a comprehensive view of the security state of your AWS resources. Security Hub collects security data from across AWS accounts and services and helps you analyze your security trends to identify and prioritize the security issues across your AWS environment.

AWS Shield Advanced is incorrect.
AWS provides AWS Shield Standard and AWS Shield Advanced for protection against

DDoS attacks. AWS Shield Standard is automatically included at no extra cost beyond what you already pay for AWS WAF and your other AWS services. For added protection against DDoS attacks, AWS offers AWS Shield Advanced.

AWS Resource Groups is incorrect. AWS Resource Groups lets you organize AWS resources such as Amazon EC2 instances, Amazon Relational Database Service databases, and Amazon S3 buckets into groups using criteria that you define as tags.

A resource group is a collection of resources that match the resource types specified in a query, and share one or more tags or portions of tags. You can create a group of resources based on their roles in your cloud infrastructure, lifecycle stages, regions, application layers, or virtually any criteria.

Resource Groups enable you to automate management tasks, such as those in AWS Systems Manager Automation documents, on tag-related resources in AWS Systems Manager.

4. Development With AWS Services

Questions

What is the primary purpose of Amazon S3 in the context of application development?

A. Hosting web applications

B. Storing and retrieving data

C. Managing containers

D. Running serverless functions

How can you trigger AWS Lambda functions in response to changes in an S3 bucket?

A. Using Amazon S3 event notifications

B. By scheduling them with Amazon CloudWatch

C. Directly from the S3 bucket properties

D. Using AWS Elastic Beanstalk

Which AWS service is designed for real-time data streaming and processing?

A. Amazon S3

B. Amazon RDS

C. Amazon Kinesis

D. AWS Lambda

What is AWS Elastic Beanstalk's role in application development?

A. Data warehousing

B. Application hosting and scaling

C. Code version control

D. Cloud security

How does AWS Elastic Beanstalk handle application scaling?

A. It automatically scales based on the number of incoming HTTP requests.

B. You manually specify the number of instances to run.

C. It uses Amazon RDS to handle scaling.

D. Scaling is not a feature of AWS Elastic Beanstalk.

Which AWS service is suitable for hosting web applications that require serverless back-end logic?

A. Amazon EC2

B. AWS Elastic Beanstalk

C. AWS Lambda

D. Amazon S3

How can you configure AWS Elastic Beanstalk to automatically deploy new versions of your application?

A. By updating the environment manually

B. By creating new environments for each version

C. By enabling automatic deployments in the environment settings

D. AWS Elastic Beanstalk does not support automatic deployments.

What is the purpose of Amazon API Gateway in application development?

A. To host web applications

B. To create, publish, and manage APIs

C. To store and retrieve data

D. To run serverless functions

What is the primary role of AWS Step Functions in application development?

A. To analyze data using SQL queries

B. To orchestrate and coordinate serverless functions

C. To host web applications

D. To manage containerized applications

Which AWS service can be used to create, publish, and manage RESTful APIs for your applications?

A. Amazon S3

B. Amazon RDS

C. Amazon API Gateway

D. Amazon Kinesis

What is the purpose of AWS App Runner in application development?

A. To monitor application performance

B. To orchestrate serverless functions

C. To easily build and deploy containerized applications

D. To store and retrieve data in real-time

Which AWS service can be used for serverless data warehousing and analytics?

A. Amazon S3

B. AWS Lambda

C. Amazon Redshift

D. AWS Elastic Beanstalk

What is AWS CodeBuild primarily used for in application development?

A. Real-time data streaming

B. Container management

C. Continuous integration and continuous deployment (CI/CD)

D. Serverless function execution

In AWS, what is the primary purpose of Amazon DynamoDB in application development?

A. Real-time data streaming

B. Database storage and retrieval

C. Application hosting

D. Code deployment

How can you invoke an AWS Lambda function from an Amazon S3 event?

A. By manually triggering it through the AWS Management Console

B. By scheduling it with Amazon CloudWatch

C. Automatically using an S3 event trigger

D. Lambda functions cannot be triggered by S3 events.

What is the primary use case for AWS Step Functions?

A. Orchestrating and coordinating multiple AWS services and functions

B. Hosting web applications

C. Data warehousing

D. Managing containers

Which AWS service can be used to create and manage containerized applications using Docker?

A. Amazon S3

B. AWS Lambda

C. Amazon ECS

D. AWS Elastic Beanstalk

What is the primary benefit of using AWS Amplify in application development?

A. Real-time data streaming

B. Serverless function execution

C. Simplified frontend and backend development

D. Container management

Which AWS service provides a fully managed data lake for analytics and data warehousing?

A. Amazon S3

B. Amazon Redshift

C. AWS Lambda

D. Amazon RDS

What is the purpose of AWS Fargate in containerized application development?

A. To manage EC2 instances

B. To create RESTful APIs

C. To easily run containers without managing the underlying infrastructure

D. To store and retrieve data in real-time

How can you ensure security in AWS Lambda functions?

A. By manually patching the operating system

B. By configuring security groups for Lambda

C. By following AWS Identity and Access Management (IAM) best practices

D. Lambda functions do not require security configurations.

What is the primary use case for AWS Glue in application development?

A. Real-time data streaming

B. Data integration and ETL (Extract, Transform, Load)

C. Serverless function execution

D. Container management

Which AWS service can be used to build and train machine learning models?

A. Amazon SageMaker

B. Amazon RDS

C. AWS Elastic Beanstalk

D. Amazon Kinesis

What is the purpose of AWS Cognito in application development?

A. To create and manage containers

B. To provide authentication and authorization for users

C. To monitor application performance

D. To store and retrieve data in real-time

Which AWS service provides a serverless computing platform that allows you to run code in response to HTTP requests?

A. Amazon EC2

B. AWS Lambda

C. Amazon S3

D. Amazon DynamoDB

How can you manage and secure API keys for authentication in Amazon API Gateway?

A. By storing them in an S3 bucket

B. By using AWS Key Management Service (KMS)

C. By encrypting them with AWS Identity and Access Management (IAM)

D. By hardcoding them in your application code

What is the primary use case for AWS Cloud9 in application development?

A. Real-time data streaming

B. Integrated development environments (IDEs)

C. Data warehousing

D. Container management

Which AWS service provides serverless computing for running code in response to pre-defined triggers?

A. Amazon S3

B. AWS Lambda

C. Amazon RDS

D. Amazon ECS

What is the purpose of AWS X-Ray in application development?

A. To analyze data using SQL queries

B. To monitor, trace, and analyze application requests

C. To host web applications

D. To create and manage containers

Which AWS service can be used to build, train, and deploy machine learning models at scale?

A. AWS Amplify

B. Amazon SageMaker

C. AWS CodeBuild

D. Amazon Redshift

Answers

Answer: B

Explanation: The primary purpose of Amazon S3 (Simple Storage Service) in the context of application development is to store and retrieve data. It provides scalable and durable object storage that can be used to store static assets, such as images, videos, and application data.

Answer: A

Explanation: AWS Lambda functions can be triggered in response to changes in an S3 bucket using Amazon S3 event notifications. You can configure S3 to send event notifications when objects are created, modified, or deleted in a bucket. Lambda functions can process these events.

Answer: C

Explanation: Amazon Kinesis is designed for real-time data streaming and processing. It allows you to ingest, process, and analyze real-time streaming data from various sources, making it suitable for applications that require real-time data insights.

Answer: B

Explanation: AWS Elastic Beanstalk's primary role in application development is to provide a platform for hosting and scaling applications. It abstracts the underlying infrastructure, making it easier to deploy and manage applications while focusing on code development.

Answer: A

Explanation: AWS Elastic Beanstalk automatically scales the number of instances based on factors like the number of incoming HTTP requests and other configurable metrics. This automatic scaling helps handle varying workloads without manual intervention.

Answer: C

Explanation: AWS Lambda is suitable for hosting serverless backend logic for web applications. It allows developers to run code in response to events (e.g., HTTP requests, S3 events) without the need to manage servers.

Answer: C

Explanation: To configure AWS Elastic Beanstalk to automatically deploy new versions of your application, you can enable automatic deployments in the environment settings. This ensures that new versions are deployed without manual intervention.

Answer: B

Explanation: The primary purpose of Amazon API Gateway in application development is to create, publish, and manage APIs for applications. It acts as a gateway that enables developers to expose APIs to clients, including mobile apps and web applications.

Answer: B

Explanation: AWS Step Functions' primary role in application development is to orchestrate and coordinate serverless functions and other AWS services. It allows you to create workflows and automate complex business processes.

Answer: C

Explanation: Amazon API Gateway can be used to create, publish, and manage RESTful APIs for your applications. It provides features like API versioning, security, and request/response transformations.

Answer: C

Explanation: AWS App Runner is used for easily building and deploying containerized applications without managing the underlying infrastructure. It streamlines the deployment process and is suitable for web applications and services.

Answer: B

Explanation: AWS Glue's primary purpose in application development is data integration and ETL (Extract, Transform, Load) for analytics and data warehousing. It simplifies data preparation and transformation tasks.

Answer: C

Explanation: AWS CodeBuild is primarily used for continuous integration and continuous deployment (CI/CD) in application development. It builds, tests, and packages your code as part of the CI/CD pipeline.

Answer: B

Explanation: In AWS, Amazon DynamoDB is a NoSQL database service primarily used for database storage and retrieval in application development. It offers high scalability and low-latency data access.

Answer: C

Explanation: You can invoke an AWS Lambda function from an Amazon S3 event automatically by configuring S3 event triggers. When specified events (e.g., object creation) occur in an S3 bucket, the Lambda function is invoked with relevant event data.

Answer: A

Explanation: AWS Step Functions are primarily used for orchestrating and coordinating multiple AWS services and functions. It allows you to create workflows with conditional logic and error handling.

Answer: C

Explanation: Amazon ECS (Elastic Container Service) can be used to create and manage containerized applications using Docker. It provides container orchestration and scaling capabilities.

Answer: C

Explanation: AWS Amplify's primary benefit in application development is simplifying frontend and backend development. It provides a set of tools and services for building full-stack applications with a focus on ease of development.

Answer: B

Explanation: Amazon Redshift is a fully managed data warehouse service for analytics and data warehousing. It allows you to run complex queries on large datasets, making it suitable for analytics workloads.

Answer: D

Explanation: AWS Fargate is used to easily run containers without managing the underlying infrastructure. It abstracts container management tasks, making it a serverless option for containerized application development.

Answer: C

Explanation: Security in AWS Lambda functions is primarily achieved by following AWS Identity and Access Management (IAM) best practices. IAM allows you to control access to Lambda functions and AWS resources securely.

Answer: B

Explanation: AWS Cognito's primary purpose in application development is to provide authentication and authorization services for users. It helps you manage user identities and access control.

Answer: B

Explanation: AWS SageMaker is primarily used to build, train, and deploy machine learning models at scale. It provides a range of machine learning tools and services.

Answer: A

Explanation: AWS X-Ray is used in application development to monitor, trace, and analyze application requests. It helps you identify performance bottlenecks and troubleshoot issues in distributed applications.

Answer: B

Explanation: AWS Lambda is used to run code in response to HTTP requests or other triggers. It provides a serverless computing platform for executing code functions.

Answer: B

Explanation: API keys in Amazon API Gateway can be secured by configuring security options and using AWS Identity and Access Management (IAM) to control access to API resources.

Answer: B

Explanation: AWS Cloud9 is used as an integrated development environment (IDE) for developing applications. It provides a cloud-based IDE with features for code editing, debugging, and collaboration.

Answer: B

Explanation: AWS Lambda provides serverless computing for running code in response to predefined triggers. It is commonly used for event-driven architecture and automation.

Answer: B

Explanation: AWS X-Ray is used to monitor, trace, and analyze application requests and distributed workflows. It provides insights into application performance and helps identify bottlenecks.

Answer: A

Explanation: AWS SageMaker is used to build, train, and deploy machine learning models at scale. It simplifies the process of developing and deploying machine learning applications.

5. Refactoring

Question

You have built a community-based app like Reddit that has millions of visitors per month. The tech stack of the app includes NodeJS, React, Redis, Amazon EC2, Amazon S3, Hadoop, Underscore, and MariaDB. Some of the community-members are complaining that the performance of the app is slowing down when the posts have engagement. Which of the following actions you can follow to resolve the issue as fast as possible with no extra cost?

(A) Use Amazon RDS Read Replicas and route read queries from your applications to the read replica

(B) Switch technology stack

(C) You can set up a read replica with its own standby instance in different AZ

(D) Set up a secure communications channel using public-key encryption between the source DB instance and the read replica

Question

After you've made your API available to be called, you realize that it needs to be optimized to improve responsiveness. After making your research you end up following the payload compression strategy. Which of the following AWS CLI command will you use to enable compression on your existing API?

(A) aws apigateway update-rest-api \

–rest-api-id 1234567890 \

–patch-operations op=replace,path=/minimumCompressionSize,value=0

(B) aws apigateway update-rest-api \

–rest-api-id 1234567890 \

–patch-operations op=replace,path=/minimumCompressionSize,value=

(C) aws apigateway update-rest-api \

–rest-api-id 1234567890 \

–patch-operations op=replace,path=/minimumCompressionSize,value=

(D) aws apigateway update-rest-api \

–patch-operations op=replace,path=/minimumCompressionSize,value=0

Question

You are building a distributed peer-to-peer file sharing application that requires low latency and scalability. The app uses a disk-based database, therefore the data retrieval speed from disk plus the added query processing times generally will put your query response times in double-digit millisecond speeds. Which of the following strategies can improve your overall application performance and reduce your database costs.

(A) Use in-memory data caching

(B) Set up origin failover

(C) Use Elastic Fabric Adapter

(D) Configure Domain Name System Security Extensions

Question

You have created a trail to enable continuous delivery of CloudTrail events to an S3 bucket, including events for CloudWatch. The Amazon S3 bucket contains more than 3,500 objects but you need to fetch and return only the first 1,000 objects in the final output without creating pagination. Which of the following options will you use to run the command

aws s3api list-objects

to meet the requirement?

(A) –page-size

(B) –max-items

(C) –cli-connect-timeout

(D) –no-paginate

Question

You are building AWS Lambda applications as it makes your Lambda projects portable and enables you to integrate with additional developer tools, such as AWS CodePipeline and AWS CodeBuild.Which of the following best practices allows you to make a more unit-testable AWS Lambda function?

(A) Separate the Lambda handler from your core logic

(B) Take advantage of execution context reuse

(C) Use a keep-alive directive

(D) Minimize your deployment package size to its runtime necessities

Question

You have an existing application that uses standard queues and you want to take advantage of the ordering and exactly-once processing features of FIFO queues. Which of the following actions needs to be done in order to convert an existing standard queue into a FIFO queue?

(A) There is an option to update the standard queue from the SQS AWS Management Console

(B) Delete your existing standard queue and recreate it as a FIFO queue

(C) Combine client-side buffering with request batching

(D) Configure a dead-letter queue

Question

For compliance purposes, you have been tasked to make sure that all of the new changes made to the items in DynamoDB are recorded and stored on another DynamoDB table in another region. What should you do in order to complete the task?

(A) Use Amazon DynamoDB Global Tables

(B) Use the Scan operation

(C) Use DynamoDB Accelerator

(D) Use DynamoDB Streams

Question

You are working on an app that starts gaining more and more traction. As a result, the user base is increasing day after day at an exponential rate. The more users the app acquired, the more delay the users experience while retrieving data from the database (DynamoDB). Now you are responsible to improve the app's performance by reducing the database response times down to microseconds. Which of the following service should you use to meet the requirement?

(A) Create a CloudFront distribution

(B) Create an Accelerators in AWS Global Accelerator

(C) Create a Classic Load Balancer

(D) Enable Amazon DynamoDB Accelerator (DAX)

Question

Your new application is hosted in an Auto Scaling group of EC2 instances. To improve the monitoring process, you have to configure it to keep the average aggregate CPU utilization of your Auto Scaling group at 50 percent. This should be done by specifying the scaling metrics and threshold values for the CloudWatch alarms that trigger the scaling process. Which of the following scaling policy type you should use?

(A) Step scaling

(B) Simple scaling

(C) Threshold scaling

(D) Target tracking scaling

Question

You are working with AWS Lambda functions and is considered as a best practice to analyze how long your function runs so that you can better determine any problems with a dependency service that may increase the concurrency of the function beyond what you expect. What function configuration should you make to determine an optimum timeout value?

(A) Performance testing your Lambda function

(B) Load test your Lambda function

(C) Minimize your deployment package size to its runtime necessities

(D) Avoid using recursive code

Question

You have created an Amazon Kinesis Data Analytics Application that process and analyze streaming data using standard SQL. When Amazon Kinesis Data Analytics inserts a row in the application stream it stores a timestamp.Which of the following types of times reflects the timestamp that is stored when a record was added to the streaming source?

(A) Event time

(B) Ingest time

(C) Processing time

(D) Streaming time

Question

You are using the extension of AWS Lambda, Lambda@Edge, as it lets you execute functions that customize the content that CloudFront delivers. You have written a Node.js function in one Region, US-East-1 (N. Virginia), and then execute this function in AWS locations globally that are closer to your viewer. Which of the following CloudFront events have to occur in order to execute the Lambda function? (Choose all that apply.)

(A) When CloudFront receives a request from a viewer (viewer request)

(B) When CloudFront receives a request from a viewer (viewer request)

(C) Before CloudFront forwards a request to the origin (origin request)

(D) Before CloudFront receives a request from a viewer (viewer request)

(E) When CloudFront receives a response from the origin (origin response)

Question

You are developing a static code using Lambda functions to automate backups and send the backups to an S3 bucket. In which of the following Init phases, the Lambda function runs the static code?

(A) Extension init

(B) Runtime init

(C) Function init

(D) Static init

Question

You are working on AWS Command Line Interface (AWS CLI) version 1 to list all objects of a given bucket. You have been noticed that when you run list commands on a large number of resources this causes calls to AWS services to exceed the maximum allowed time and generate a "timed out" errors. What action you can take to resolve this issue??

(A) Use the –page-size option to request a smaller number of items from each call to the AWS service

(B) Type the 'aws ec2 help' AWS CLI command

(C) Use the client-side pager program for output

(D) Update to the latest version of the AWS CLI version 2

Question

You are developing an application that uses CloudFront to speed up the distribution of the web content and to keep the content secure while in transit. Which of the following ways you can use CloudFront to secure and restrict access to content? (Choose all that apply.)

(A) Configure HTTP connections

(B) Require users to access content using CloudFront signed URLs

(C) Use AWS Shield to control access to your content

(D) Set up field-level encryption for specific content fields

(E) Prevent users in specific geographic locations from accessing content

Question

Suppose that you have a large customer base spread across three geographic areas—the US East Coast, the US West Coast, and Western Europe. Customers can update their profile information using your application. To satisfy this use case, you need to create three identical DynamoDB tables named CustomerProfiles, in three different AWS Regions where the customers are located. What should you do to replicate data changes among these tables without writing your own code?

(A) Use DynamoDB Accelerator (DAX)

(B) Use NoSQL Workbench

(C) Use DynamoDB Global tables

(D) Use point-in-time recovery

Question

You have been tasked to implement the following scenario. Each time an item in the table is modified and a new record appears in the table's stream then copy each stream record to persistent storage, such as Amazon Simple Storage Service (Amazon S3), to create a permanent audit. Which of the following action should you take to meet the requirement?

(A) Enable DynamoDB Streams and AWS Lambda Triggers

(B) Use the DynamoDB Streams Kinesis Adapter

(C) Use Global Secondary Indexes

(D) Use the Scan operation in Amazon DynamoDB

Question

The AWS account of the ExamsDigest has an ID of 318855545211. The sign-in page URL has the following format https://318855545211.signin.aws.amazon.com/console. We want the URL for our sign-in page to contain our company name (ExamsDigest) instead of the AWS account ID. Which of the following AWS CLI command will you use to create an alias?

(A) iam create-account-alias –account-alias examsdigest

(B) aws iam list-account-aliases

(C) aws iam create-account-alias –account-alias examsdigest

(D) aws iam list-account-aliases examsdigest

Question

What can you accomplish if you use an ElastiCache for Memcached cluster to store the user session state of the application?

(A) Allow you to route a site user to the particular web server that is managing that individual user's session

(B) Boost the overall performance of your applications

(C) Speed up the distribution of your static and dynamic web content

(D) Centrally manage users and security credentials

Question

You want to configure CloudFront to use HTTPS to communicate with your origin Amazon S3 for encrypted connection between CloudFront and Amazon S3. What action should you take to meet the requirement?

(A) Use a MediaStore Container

(B) Create a CloudFront distribution

(C) Change the value of the Viewer Protocol Policy

(D) Set up field-level encryption for specific content fields

Answers

Question

You have built a community-based app like Reddit that has millions of visitors per month. The tech stack of the app includes NodeJS, React, Redis, Amazon EC2, Amazon S3, Hadoop, Underscore, and MariaDB. Some of the community-members are complaining that the performance of the app is slowing down when the posts have engagement. Which of the following actions you can follow to resolve the issue as fast as possible with no extra cost?

(A) Use Amazon RDS Read Replicas and route read queries from your applications to the read replica

(B) Switch technology stack

(C) You can set up a read replica with its own standby instance in different AZ

(D) Set up a secure communications channel using public-key encryption between the source DB instance and the read replica

Explanation

Use Amazon RDS Read Replicas and route read queries from your applications to the read replica is the correct answer.

Amazon RDS Read Replicas provide enhanced performance and durability for RDS database (DB) instances. They make it easy to elastically scale out beyond the capacity constraints of a single DB instance for read-heavy database workloads.

You can create one or more replicas of a given source DB Instance and serve high-volume application read traffic from multiple copies of your data, thereby increasing aggregate read throughput.

You can reduce the load on your source DB instance by routing read queries from your applications to the read replica.

Switch technology stack is incorrect

because switching the tech stack indeed can affect the performance but in our case, we use advanced technologies and switching the tech can cost too much money and time.

You can set up a read replica with its own standby instance in different AZ is incorrect

because this action increases the availability of the app.

Set up a secure communications channel using public-key encryption between the source DB instance and the read replica is incorrect

because this action increases the security of the app.

Question

After you've made your API available to be called, you realize that it needs to be optimized to improve responsiveness. After making your research you end up following the payload compression strategy. Which of the following AWS CLI command will you use to enable compression on your existing API?

(A) aws apigateway update-rest-api \

–rest-api-id 1234567890 \

–patch-operations op=replace,path=/minimumCompressionSize,value=0

(B) aws apigateway update-rest-api \

–rest-api-id 1234567890 \

–patch-operations op=replace,path=/minimumCompressionSize,value=

(C) aws apigateway update-rest-api \

–rest-api-id 1234567890 \

–patch-operations op=replace,path=/minimumCompressionSize,value=

(D) aws apigateway update-rest-api \

–patch-operations op=replace,path=/minimumCompressionSize,value=0

Explanation

**The correct answer is: aws apigateway update-rest-api **

**–rest-api-id 1234567890 **

–patch-operations op=replace,path=/minimumCompressionSize,value=0

After you've made your API available to be called, you might realize that it needs to be optimized to improve responsiveness. API Gateway provides a few strategies for optimizing your API, like response caching and payload compression.

You can enable compression for an API using the API Gateway console, the AWS CLI, or an AWS SDK. For an existing API, you must deploy the API after enabling the compression in order for the change to take effect. For a new API, you can deploy the API after the API setup is complete.

Question

You are building a distributed peer-to-peer file sharing application that requires low latency and scalability. The app uses a disk-based database, therefore the data retrieval speed from disk plus the added query processing times generally will put your query response times in double-digit millisecond speeds. Which of the following strategies can improve your overall application performance and reduce your database costs.

(A) Use in-memory data caching

(B) Set up origin failover

(C) Use Elastic Fabric Adapter

(D) Configure Domain Name System Security Extensions

Explanation

Use in-memory data caching is the correct answer.

In-memory data caching can be one of the most effective strategies to improve your overall application performance and to reduce your database costs.

Caching can be applied to any type of database including relational databases such as Amazon RDS or NoSQL databases such as Amazon DynamoDB, MongoDB and Apache Cassandra. The best part of caching is that it's minimally invasive to implement and by doing so, your application performance regarding both scale and speed is dramatically improved.

Set up origin failover is incorrect.

You can set up CloudFront with origin failover for scenarios that require high availability.

Use Elastic Fabric Adapter (EFA) is incorrect

. An Elastic Fabric Adapter (EFA) is a network device that you can attach to your Amazon EC2 instance to accelerate High-Performance Computing (HPC) and machine learning applications.

Configure Domain Name System Security Extensions is incorrect.

Attackers sometimes hijack traffic to internet endpoints such as web servers by intercepting DNS queries and returning their own IP addresses to DNS resolvers in place of the actual IP addresses for those endpoints. Users are then routed to the IP addresses provided by the attackers in the spoofed response, for example, to fake websites.

You can protect your domain from this type of attack, known as DNS spoofing or a man-in-the-middle attack, by configuring Domain Name System Security Extensions (DNSSEC), a protocol for securing DNS traffic.

Question

You have created a trail to enable continuous delivery of CloudTrail events to an S3 bucket, including events for CloudWatch. The Amazon S3 bucket contains more than 3,500 objects but you need to fetch and return only the first 1,000 objects in the final output without creating pagination. Which of the following options will you use to run the command

aws s3api list-objects

to meet the requirement?

(A) –page-size

(B) –max-items

(C) –cli-connect-timeout

(D) –no-paginate

Explanation

–no-paginate is the correct answer.

By default, the AWS CLI uses a page size of 1000 and retrieves all available items. For example, if you run

aws s3api list-objects

on an Amazon S3 bucket that contains 3,500 objects, the AWS CLI automatically makes four calls to Amazon S3, handling the service-specific pagination logic for you in the background and returning all 3,500 objects in the final output.

To disable pagination and return only the first page of results, use the

--no-paginate

option. When using a command, by default the AWS CLI automatically makes multiple calls to return all possible results to create pagination. One call for each page. Disabling pagination has the AWS CLI only call once for the first page of command results.

For example, if you run

aws s3api list-objects

on an Amazon S3 bucket that contains 3,500 objects, the AWS CLI only makes the first call to Amazon S3, returning only the first 1,000 objects in the final output

–page-size is incorrect.

You can use the

--page-size

option to specify that the AWS CLI request a smaller number of items from each call to the AWS service. The CLI still retrieves the full list, but performs a larger number of service API calls in the background and retrieves a smaller number of items with each call. This gives the individual calls a better chance of succeeding without a timeout. The –page-size can be technically correct but the question says to retrieve only the first 1,000 objects without creating pagination

–max-items is incorrect.

To include fewer items at a time in the AWS CLI output, use the –max-items option. The AWS CLI still handles pagination with the service as described previously, but prints out only the number of items at a time that you specify.

–

cli-connect-timeout is incorrect.

It's an AWS CLI command that specifies the maximum socket connect time in seconds.

Question

You are building AWS Lambda applications as it makes your Lambda projects portable and enables you to integrate with additional developer tools, such as AWS CodePipeline and AWS CodeBuild. Which of the following best practices allows you to make a more unit-testable AWS Lambda function?

(A) Separate the Lambda handler from your core logic

(B) Take advantage of execution context reuse

(C) Use a keep-alive directive

(D) Minimize your deployment package size to its runtime necessities

Explanation

Separate the Lambda handler from your core logic is the correct answer.

This allows you to make a more unit-testable function. In Node.js this may look like:

Take advantage of execution context reuse is incorrect because this improves the performance of your function.

Use a keep-alive directive is incorrect

because this maintain persistent connections. Lambda purges idle connections over time. Attempting to reuse an idle connection when invoking a function will result in a connection error. To maintain your persistent connection, use the keep-alive directive associated with your runtime.

Minimize your deployment package size to its runtime necessities is incorrect this will reduce the amount of time that it takes for your deployment package to be downloaded and unpacked ahead of invocation.

Question

You have an existing application that uses standard queues and you want to take advantage of the ordering and exactly-once processing features of FIFO queues. Which of the following actions needs to be done in order to convert an existing standard queue into a FIFO queue?

(A) There is an option to update the standard queue from the SQS AWS Management Console

(B) Delete your existing standard queue and recreate it as a FIFO queue

(C) Combine client-side buffering with request batching

(D) Configure a dead-letter queue

Explanation Delete your existing standard queue and recreate it as a FIFO queue is the correct answer.

Amazon SQS offers standard as the default queue type. Standard queues support a nearly unlimited number of API calls per second, per API action (SendMessage, ReceiveMessage, or DeleteMessage).

FIFO (First-In-First-Out)

queues are designed to enhance messaging between applications when the order of operations and events is critical, or where duplicates can't be tolerated, for example:

1.Ensure that user-entered commands are executed in the right order.

2. Display the correct product price by sending price modifications in the right order.

3.Display the correct product price by sending price modifications in the right order.

If you have an existing application that uses standard queues and you want to take advantage of the ordering or exactly-once processing features of FIFO queues, you need to configure the queue and your application correctly.

You can't convert an existing standard queue into a FIFO queue. To make the move, you must either create a new FIFO queue for your application or delete your existing standard queue and recreate it as a FIFO queue.

There is an option to update the standard queue from the SQS AWS Management Console is incorrect

because the only way to make the conversion is to either create a new FIFO queue for your application or delete your existing standard queue and recreate it as a FIFO queue.

Combine client-side buffering with request batching is incorrect

because this action can reduce the Amazon SQS costs.

Configure a dead-letter queue is incorrect

because this action is useful for debugging your application or messaging system by isolating problematic messages to determine why the processing doesn't succeed.

Question

For compliance purposes, you have been tasked to make sure that all of the new changes made to the items in DynamoDB are recorded and stored on another DynamoDB table in another region. What should you do in order to complete the task?

(A) Use Amazon DynamoDB Global Tables

(B) Use the Scan operation

(C) Use DynamoDB Accelerator

(D) Use DynamoDB Streams

Explanation

Use DynamoDB Streams is the correct answer.

Many applications can benefit from the ability to capture changes to items stored in a DynamoDB table, at the point in time when such changes occur.

The following are some example use cases:

An application in one AWS Region modifies the data in a DynamoDB table. A second application in another Region reads these data modifications and writes the data to another table, creating a replica that stays in sync with the original table.

A popular mobile app modifies data in a DynamoDB table, at the rate of thousands of updates per second. Another application captures and stores data about these updates, providing near-real-time usage metrics for the mobile app.

A global multi-player game has a multi-active topology, storing data in multiple AWS Regions. Each locale stays in sync by consuming and replaying the changes that occur in the remote Regions.

An application automatically sends notifications to the mobile devices of all friends in a group as soon as one friend uploads a new picture.

A new customer adds data to a DynamoDB table. This event invokes another application that sends a welcome email to the new customer.

DynamoDB Streams enables solutions such as these, and many others. DynamoDB Streams captures a time-ordered sequence of item-level modifications in any DynamoDB table and stores this information in a log for up to 24 hours. Applications can access this log and view the data items as they appeared before and after they were modified, in near-real time.

Use Amazon DynamoDB Global Tables is incorrect

because Global Tables provide a fully managed solution for deploying a multi-region, multi-active database, without having to build and maintain your own replication solution.

Use the Scan operation is incorrect

because a Scan operation in Amazon DynamoDB reads every item in a table or a secondary index. By default, a Scan operation returns all of the data attributes for every item in the table or index.

Use DynamoDB Accelerator is incorrect

because DynamoDB Accelerator (DAX) delivers fast response times for accessing eventually consistent data. DAX is a DynamoDB-compatible caching service that enables you to benefit from fast in-memory performance for demanding applications.

Question

You are working on an app that starts gaining more and more traction. As a result, the user base is increasing day after day at an exponential rate. The more users the app acquired, the more delay the users experience while retrieving data from the database (DynamoDB). Now you are responsible to improve the app's performance by reducing the database response times down to microseconds. Which of the following service should you use to meet the requirement?

(A) Create a CloudFront distribution

(B) Create an Accelerators in AWS Global Accelerator

(C) Create a Classic Load Balancer

(D) Enable Amazon DynamoDB Accelerator (DAX)

Explanation Enable Amazon DynamoDB Accelerator (DAX) is the correct answer.

Amazon DynamoDB Accelerator (DAX) is a fully managed, highly available, in-memory cache for Amazon DynamoDB that delivers up to a 10 times performance improvement—from milliseconds to microseconds—even at millions of requests per second.

DAX does all the heavy lifting required to add in-memory acceleration to your DynamoDB tables, without requiring developers to manage cache invalidation, data population, or cluster management.

Now you can focus on building great applications for your customers without worrying about performance at scale. You do not need to modify application logic because DAX is compatible with existing DynamoDB API calls.

Create a CloudFront distribution is incorrect.

You create a CloudFront distribution to tell CloudFront where you want content to be delivered from, and the details about how to track and manage content delivery. In our case, the issue is database-related and not CDN-related.

Create an Accelerators in AWS Global Accelerator is incorrect.

An accelerator in AWS Global Accelerator directs traffic to optimal endpoints over the AWS global network to improve the availability and performance of your internet applications that have a global audience.

Create a Classic Load Balancer is incorrect.

A load balancer distributes incoming application traffic across multiple EC2 instances in multiple Availability Zones. This increases the fault tolerance of your applications. Elastic Load Balancing detects unhealthy instances and routes traffic only to healthy instances.

Question

Your new application is hosted in an Auto Scaling group of EC2 instances. To improve the monitoring process, you have to configure it to keep the average aggregate CPU utilization of your Auto Scaling group at 50 percent. This should be done by specifying the scaling metrics and threshold values for the CloudWatch alarms that trigger the scaling process. Which of the following scaling policy type you should use?

(A) Step scaling

(B) Simple scaling

(C) Threshold scaling

(D) Target tracking scaling

Explanation Target tracking scaling is the correct answer.

With

target tracking scaling policies,

you select a scaling metric and set a target value. Amazon EC2 Auto Scaling creates and manages the CloudWatch alarms that trigger the scaling policy and calculates the scaling adjustment based on the metric and the target value. The scaling policy adds or removes capacity as required to keep the metric at, or close to, the specified target value. In addition to keeping the metric close to the target value, a target tracking scaling policy also adjusts to changes in the metric due to a changing load pattern.

For example, you can use target tracking scaling to:

Configure a target tracking scaling policy to keep the average aggregate CPU utilization of your Auto Scaling group at 50 percent.

Question

You are working with AWS Lambda functions and is considered as a best practice to analyze how long your function runs so that you can better determine any problems with a dependency service that may increase the concurrency of the function beyond what you expect. What function configuration should you make to determine an optimum timeout value?

(A) Performance testing your Lambda function

(B) Load test your Lambda function

(C) Minimize your deployment package size to its runtime necessities

(D) Avoid using recursive code

Explanation Load test your Lambda function is the correct answer.

Load test your Lambda function to determine an optimum timeout value. It is important to analyze how long your function runs so that you can better determine any problems with a dependency service that may increase the concurrency of the function beyond what you expect. This is especially important when your Lambda function makes network calls to resources that may not handle Lambda's scaling.

Performance testing your Lambda function is incorrect.

Performance testing your Lambda function is a crucial part in ensuring you pick the optimum memory size configuration. Any increase in memory size triggers an equivalent increase in CPU available to your function.

Minimize your deployment package size to its runtime necessities is incorrect.

This will reduce the amount of time that it takes for your deployment package to be downloaded and unpacked ahead of invocation.

Avoid using recursive code is incorrect.

Avoid using recursive code in your Lambda function, wherein the function automatically calls itself until some arbitrary criteria are met. This could lead to an unintended volume of function invocations and escalated costs.

Question

You have created an Amazon Kinesis Data Analytics Application that process and analyze streaming data using standard SQL. When Amazon Kinesis Data Analytics inserts a row in the application stream it stores a timestamp.

Which of the following types of times reflects the timestamp that is stored when a record was added to the streaming source?

(A) Event time

(B) Ingest time

(C) Processing time

(D) Streaming time

Explanation Ingest time is the correct answer.

With Amazon Kinesis Data Analytics for SQL Applications, you can process and analyze streaming data using standard SQL. The service enables you to quickly author and run powerful SQL code against streaming sources to perform time-series analytics, feed real-time dashboards, and create real-time metrics.

There are types of times in real-time streaming applications. These are:

Event time

– The timestamp when the event occurred. This is also sometimes called the client-side time. It is often desirable to use this time in analytics because it is the time when an event occurred. However, many event sources, such as mobile phones and web clients, do not have reliable clocks, which can lead to inaccurate times. In addition, connectivity issues can lead to records appearing on a stream not in the same order the events occurred.

Ingest time

– The timestamp of when record was added to the streaming source. Amazon Kinesis Data Streams includes a field called APPROXIMATE_ARRIVAL_TIME in every record that provides this timestamp. This is also sometimes referred to as the server-side time. This ingest time is often the close approximation of event time. If there is any kind of delay in the record ingestion to the stream, this can lead to inaccuracies, which are typically rare. Also, the ingest time is rarely out of order, but it can occur due to the distributed nature of streaming data. Therefore, Ingest time is a mostly accurate and in-order reflection of the event time.

Processing time

– The timestamp when Amazon Kinesis Data Analytics inserts a row in the first in-application stream. Amazon Kinesis Data Analytics provides this timestamp in the ROWTIME column that exists in each in-application stream.

Streaming time is incorrect

as this is not a valid type of times in real-time streaming applications.

Question

You are using the extension of AWS Lambda, Lambda@Edge, as it lets you execute functions that customize the content that CloudFront delivers. You have written a Node.js function in one Region, US-East-1 (N. Virginia), and then execute this function in AWS locations globally that are closer to your viewer. Which of the following CloudFront events have to occur in order to execute the Lambda function? (Choose all that apply.)

(A) When CloudFront receives a request from a viewer (viewer request)

(B) When CloudFront receives a request from a viewer (viewer request)

(C) Before CloudFront forwards a request to the origin (origin request)

(D) Before CloudFront receives a request from a viewer (viewer request)

(E) When CloudFront receives a response from the origin (origin response)

Explanation The correct answers are:

1. When CloudFront receives a request from a viewer (viewer request)

2. Before CloudFront forwards a request to the origin (origin request)

3. When CloudFront receives a response from the origin (origin response)

Lambda@Edge is an extension of AWS Lambda, a compute service that lets you execute functions that customize the content that CloudFront delivers. You can author Node.js or Python functions in one Region, US-East-1 (N. Virginia), and then execute them in AWS locations globally that are closer to the viewer, without provisioning or managing servers. Lambda@Edge scales automatically, from a few requests per day to thousands per second. Processing requests at AWS locations closer to the viewer instead of on origin servers significantly reduces latency and improves the user experience.

When you associate a CloudFront distribution with a Lambda@Edge function, CloudFront intercepts requests and responses at CloudFront edge locations.

You can execute Lambda functions when the following CloudFront events occur:

1. When CloudFront receives a request from a viewer (viewer request)

2. Before CloudFront forwards a request to the origin (origin request)

3. When CloudFront receives a response from the origin (origin response)

4. Before CloudFront returns the response to the viewer (viewer response)

Question

You are developing a static code using Lambda functions to automate backups and send the backups to an S3 bucket. In which of the following Init phases, the Lambda function runs the static code?

(A) Extension init

(B) Runtime init

(C) Function init

(D) Static init

Explanation

Function init is the correct answer.

The lifecycle of the execution environment includes the following phases:

Init:

In this phase, Lambda creates or unfreezes an execution environment with the configured resources, downloads the code for the function and all layers, initializes any extensions, initializes the runtime, and then runs the function's initialization code. The

Init

phase is split into three sub-phases:

Extension init

,

Runtime init

and

Function init

Invoke:

In this phase, Lambda invokes the function handler. After the function runs to completion, Lambda prepares to handle another function invocation.

Shutdown:

This phase is triggered if the Lambda function does not receive any invokes for a period of time.

In the

Init

phase, Lambda performs three tasks:

Start all extensions (

Extension init

)

Bootstrap the runtime (

Runtime init

)

Run the function's static code (

Function init

)

Question

You are working on AWS Command Line Interface (AWS CLI) version 1 to list all objects of a given bucket. You have been noticed that when you run list commands on a large number of resources this causes calls to AWS services to exceed the maximum allowed time and generate a "timed out" errors. What action you can take to resolve this issue??

(A) Use the –page-size option to request a smaller number of items from each call to the AWS service

(B) Type the 'aws ec2 help' AWS CLI command

(C) Use the client-side pager program for output

(D) Update to the latest version of the AWS CLI version 2

Explanation

Use the –page-size option to request a smaller number of items from each call to the AWS service.

If you see issues when running list commands on a large number of resources, the default page size of 1000 might be too high. This can cause calls to AWS services to exceed the maximum allowed time and generate a “timed out” error.

You can use the

--page-size

option to specify that the AWS CLI requests a smaller number of items from each call to the AWS service. The CLI still retrieves the full list but performs a larger number of service API calls in the background and retrieves a smaller number of items with each call. This gives the individual calls a better chance of succeeding without a timeout. Changing the page size doesn’t affect the output; it affects only the number of API calls that need to be made to generate the output.

Type the ‘aws ec2 help’ AWS CLI command is incorrect

because the command displays the available Amazon Elastic Compute Cloud (Amazon EC2) specific commands.

Use the client-side pager program for output is incorrect

because this feature is available only with AWS CLI version 2 and by default, this feature returns all output through your operating system’s default pager program.

Update to the latest version of the AWS CLI version 2 is incorrect

because updating to AWL CLI v2 can’t resolve the “timed out” errors.

Question 75.

You are developing an application that uses CloudFront to speed up the distribution of the web content and to keep the content secure while in transit. Which of the following ways you can use CloudFront to secure and restrict access to content? (Choose all that apply.)

(A) Configure HTTP connections

(B) Require users to access content using CloudFront signed URLs

(C) Use AWS Shield to control access to your content

(D) Set up field-level encryption for specific content fields

(E) Prevent users in specific geographic locations from accessing content

Explanation The correct answers are:

1. Require users to access content using CloudFront signed URLs

2. Set up field-level encryption for specific content fields

3. Prevent users in specific geographic locations from accessing content

Amazon CloudFront is a web service that speeds up the distribution of your static and dynamic web content, such as .html, .css, .js, and image files, to your users. CloudFront delivers your content through a worldwide network of data centers called edge locations. When a user requests content that you're serving with CloudFront, the user is routed to the edge location that provides the lowest latency (time delay), so that content is delivered with the best possible performance.

If the content is already in the edge location with the lowest latency, CloudFront delivers it immediately.

If the content is not in that edge location, CloudFront retrieves it from an origin that you've defined—such as an Amazon S3 bucket, a MediaPackage channel, or an HTTP server (for example, a web server) that you have identified as the source for the definitive version of your content.

For web distributions, CloudFront provides several options for securing content that it delivers. The following are some ways you can use CloudFront to secure and restrict access to content:

1. Configure HTTPS connections

2. Prevent users in specific geographic locations from accessing content

3.Require users to access content using CloudFront signed URLs or signed cookies

4.Set up field-level encryption for specific content fields

5.Use AWS WAF to control access to your content

Configure HTTP connections is incorrect

because to secure and restrict access to content requires to configure HTTPS connections.

Use AWS Shield to control access to your content is incorrect

because AWS provides protection against DDoS attacks. To control access to your content you can use AWS WAF.

Question

Suppose that you have a large customer base spread across three geographic areas—the US East Coast, the US West Coast, and Western Europe. Customers can update their profile information using your application. To satisfy this use case, you need to create three identical DynamoDB tables named CustomerProfiles, in three different AWS Regions where the customers are located. What should you do to replicate data changes among these tables without writing your own code?

(A) Use DynamoDB Accelerator (DAX)

(B) Use NoSQL Workbench

(C) Use DynamoDB Global tables

(D) Use point-in-time recovery

Explanation Use DynamoDB Global tables is the correct answer.

Amazon DynamoDB global tables provide a fully managed solution for deploying a multiregion, multi-active database, without having to build and maintain your own replication solution. With global tables you can specify the AWS Regions where you want the table to be available. DynamoDB performs all of the necessary tasks to create identical tables in these Regions and propagate ongoing data changes to all of them.

Use DynamoDB Accelerator (DAX) is incorrect.

Amazon DynamoDB is designed for scale and performance. In most cases, the DynamoDB response times can be measured in single-digit milliseconds. However, there are certain use cases that require response times in microseconds. For these use cases, DynamoDB Accelerator (DAX) delivers fast response times for accessing eventually consistent data.

DAX is a DynamoDB-compatible caching service that enables you to benefit from fast in-memory performance for demanding applications.

Use NoSQL Workbench is incorrect.

NoSQL Workbench for Amazon DynamoDB is a cross-platform client-side GUI application for modern database development and operations and is available for Windows, macOS, and Linux. NoSQL Workbench is a unified visual IDE tool that provides data modeling, data visualization, and query development features to help you design, create, query, and manage DynamoDB tables.

Use point-in-time recovery is incorrect.

Point-in-time recovery helps protect your DynamoDB tables from accidental write or delete operations. With point-in-time recovery, you don't have to worry about creating, maintaining, or scheduling on-demand backups.

Question

You have been tasked to implement the following scenario. Each time an item in the table is modified and a new record appears in the table's stream then copy each stream record to persistent storage, such as Amazon Simple Storage Service (Amazon S3), to create a permanent audit. Which of the following action should you take to meet the requirement?

(A) Enable DynamoDB Streams and AWS Lambda Triggers

(B) Use the DynamoDB Streams Kinesis Adapter

(C) Use Global Secondary Indexes

(D) Use the Scan operation in Amazon DynamoDB

Explanation

Enable DynamoDB Streams and AWS Lambda Triggers is the correct answer.

Amazon DynamoDB is integrated with AWS Lambda so that you can create triggers—pieces of code that automatically respond to events in DynamoDB Streams.

If you enable DynamoDB Streams on a table, you can associate the stream Amazon Resource Name (ARN) with an AWS Lambda function that you write. Immediately after an item in the table is modified, a new record appears in the table's stream. AWS Lambda polls the stream and invokes your Lambda function synchronously when it detects new stream records.

The Lambda function can perform any actions you specify, such as sending a notification or initiating a workflow. For example, you can write a Lambda function to simply copy each stream record to persistent storage, such as Amazon Simple Storage Service (Amazon S3), to create a permanent audit trail of write activity in your table.

Use the DynamoDB Streams Kinesis Adapter is incorrect.

Using the Amazon Kinesis Adapter is the recommended way to consume streams from Amazon DynamoDB.

Use Global Secondary Indexes is incorrect.

Global Secondary Indexes are used to perform many kinds of queries, using a variety of different attributes as query criteria in DynamoDB.

Use the Scan operation in Amazon DynamoDB is incorrect.

A Scan operation in Amazon DynamoDB reads every item in a table or a secondary index. By default, a Scan operation returns all of the data attributes for every item in the table or index.

Question

The AWS account of the ExamsDigest has an ID of 318855545211. The sign-in page URL has the following format https://318855545211.signin.aws.amazon.com/console. We want the URL for our sign-in page to contain our company name (ExamsDigest) instead of the AWS account ID. Which of the following AWS CLI command will you use to create an alias?

(A) iam create-account-alias –account-alias examsdigest

(B) aws iam list-account-aliases

(C) aws iam create-account-alias –account-alias examsdigest

(D) aws iam list-account-aliases examsdigest

Explanation aws iam create-account-alias –account-alias examsdigest is the correct answer.

If you want the URL for your sign-in page to contain your company name (or other friendly identifier) instead of your AWS account ID, you can create an account alias.

Your sign-in page URL has the following format, by default.

https://Your_Account_ID.signin.aws.amazon.com/console

If you create an AWS account alias for your AWS account ID, your sign-in page URL looks like the following example.

https://Your_Account_Alias.signin.aws.amazon.com/console

The original URL containing your AWS account ID remains active and can be used after you create your AWS account alias.

To create an alias for your AWS Management Console sign-in page URL, run the following command:

aws iam create-account-alias --account-alias Your_Account_Alias

iam create-account-alias –account-alias examsdigest is incorrect

because it's missing the aws in front.

aws iam list-account-aliases is incorrect

because this command displays your AWS account ID alias.

aws iam list-account-aliases examsdigest is incorrect

because the command aws iam list-account-aliases doesn't accept parameters and this command displays your AWS account ID alias.

Question

What can you accomplish if you use an ElastiCache for Memcached cluster to store the user session state of the application?

(A) Allow you to route a site user to the particular web server that is managing that individual user's session

(B) Boost the overall performance of your applications

(C) Speed up the distribution of your static and dynamic web content

(D) Centrally manage users and security credentials

Explanation Boost the overall performance of your applications is the correct answer.

There are various ways to manage user sessions including storing those sessions locally to the node responding to the HTTP request or designating a layer in your architecture which can store those sessions in a scalable and robust manner.

In order to address scalability and to provide a shared data storage for sessions that can be accessible from any individual web server, you can abstract the HTTP sessions from the web servers themselves. A common solution to for this is to leverage an In-Memory Key/Value store such as Redis and Memcached.

While Key/Value data stores are known to be extremely fast and provide sub-millisecond latency, the added network latency and added cost are the drawbacks. An added benefit of leveraging Key/Value stores is that they can also be utilized to cache any data, not just HTTP sessions, which can help boost the overall performance of your applications.

Allow you to route a site user to the particular web server that is managing that individual user's session is incorrect

because this is a different approach to manage user sessions known as session affinity.

Speed up the distribution of your static and dynamic web content is incorrect

because this is a feature from Amazon CloudFront.

Centrally manage users and security credentials is incorrect

because this is a feature from AWS Identity and Access Management.

Question

You want to configure CloudFront to use HTTPS to communicate with your origin Amazon S3 for encrypted connection between CloudFront and Amazon S3. What action should you take to meet the requirement?

(A) Use a MediaStore Container

(B) Create a CloudFront distribution

(C) Change the value of the Viewer Protocol Policy

(D) Set up field-level encryption for specific content fields

Explanation

Change the value of the Viewer Protocol Policy is the correct answer.

If you want to require HTTPS for communication between CloudFront and Amazon S3, you must change the value of

Viewer Protocol Policy to Redirect HTTP to HTTPS or HTTPS Only.

When you use HTTPS with an Amazon S3 bucket that supports HTTPS communication, Amazon S3 provides the SSL/TLS certificate, so you don't have to.

To configure CloudFront to require HTTPS to your Amazon S3 origin

1. Sign in to the AWS Management Console and open the CloudFront console at

https://console.aws.amazon.com/cloudfront/.

2.In the top pane of the CloudFront console, choose the ID for the distribution that you want to update.

3.On the Behaviors tab, choose the cache behavior that you want to update, and then choose Edit.

4.Specify one of the following values for Viewer Protocol Policy:

Redirect HTTP to HTTPS

Viewers can use both protocols, but HTTP requests are automatically redirected to HTTPS requests. CloudFront returns HTTP status code 301 (Moved Permanently) along with the new HTTPS URL. The viewer then resubmits the request to CloudFront using the HTTPS URL.

When a viewer makes an HTTP request that is redirected to an HTTPS request, CloudFront charges for both requests.

HTTPS Only

Viewers can access your content only if they're using HTTPS. If a viewer sends an HTTP request instead of an HTTPS request, CloudFront returns HTTP status code 403 (Forbidden) and does not return the object.

5. Choose Yes, Edit.

6.Repeat steps 3 through 5 for each additional cache behavior that you want to require HTTPS for between viewers and CloudFront, and between CloudFront and S3.

7.Confirm the following before you use the updated configuration in a production environment:

- The path pattern in each cache behavior applies only to the requests that you want viewers to use HTTPS for.

- The cache behaviors are listed in the order that you want CloudFront to evaluate them in.

- The cache behaviors are routing requests to the correct origins.

Use a MediaStore Container is incorrect.

To stream video by using CloudFront, you can set up an Amazon S3 bucket that is configured as a MediaStore container, or create a channel and endpoints with MediaPackage.

Create a CloudFront distribution is incorrect.

You create a CloudFront distribution to tell CloudFront where you want content to be delivered from, and the details about how to track and manage content delivery.

Set up field-level encryption for specific content fields is incorrect.

This is a CloudFront option to secure and restrict access to content.

Conclusion

AWS offers a vast array of services and tools that empower developers to build, deploy, and manage applications efficiently and effectively. This chapter covered various aspects of development with AWS services, from serverless computing with AWS Lambda to container management with Amazon ECS and AWS Fargate. AWS Elastic Beanstalk simplifies application hosting and scaling, while services like Amazon S3, DynamoDB, and RDS provide data storage and retrieval capabilities.

AWS provides solutions for real-time data streaming, orchestration of serverless functions using AWS Step Functions, and creating, publishing, and managing APIs with Amazon API Gateway. The platform also supports machine learning development with services like Amazon SageMaker and offers tools for continuous integration and continuous deployment (CI/CD), such as AWS CodeBuild and AWS CodePipeline.

Security and monitoring are essential components of AWS development, with services like AWS Identity and Access Management (IAM), AWS X-Ray, and AWS CloudWatch ensuring the security and performance of applications.

In the ever-evolving landscape of cloud computing, AWS continues to innovate and expand its offerings to meet the diverse needs of developers and organizations. By leveraging the capabilities of AWS services, developers can build scalable, secure, and highly available applications that drive innovation and business growth.

Congratulations! You have completed this comprehensive guide to preparing for the AWS Certified Developer exam. In this book, we have covered essential topics related to AWS services, exam preparation strategies, practice test questions, and detailed answers to help you succeed in your certification journey.

AWS Certified Developer certification validates your skills and knowledge in developing applications on the Amazon Web Services (AWS) platform. By earning this certification, you demonstrate your ability to design, deploy, and maintain scalable and reliable applications on AWS.

Throughout this book, we emphasized the importance of practice tests in your exam preparation. These practice questions and answers have been designed to help you assess your knowledge, identify areas for improvement, and build confidence for the actual exam. We encourage you to use these practice tests as a valuable resource in your study plan.

Remember that success in the AWS Certified Developer exam requires a combination of theoretical understanding and practical experience. It's essential to not only grasp the concepts but also to practice applying them to real-world scenarios. AWS provides a wealth of resources, including documentation, tutorials, and hands-on labs, to help you gain practical experience with AWS services.

As you continue your preparation, keep the following key points in mind:

Hands-On Experience: Practice using AWS services by working on real projects or lab exercises. The more you interact with AWS, the more confident you will become in using the platform effectively.

Study Resources: Utilize a variety of study resources, including AWS documentation, online courses, official AWS practice exams, and community forums. These resources provide different perspectives and insights into AWS services.

Exam Objectives: Familiarize yourself with the AWS Certified Developer exam objectives outlined in the official exam guide. Ensure that your study plan aligns with the topics and domains covered in the exam.

Time Management: Plan your study schedule to allocate sufficient time for each exam domain. Practice time management during the exam to ensure you complete all questions within the allocated time.

Continuous Learning: AWS is a dynamic and evolving platform. Stay updated on the latest AWS services, best practices, and architectural patterns to enhance your skills even after passing the certification exam.

Lastly, remember that earning the AWS Certified Developer certification is a significant achievement that can open doors to exciting career opportunities. Whether you are a developer, DevOps engineer, or solutions architect, AWS skills are highly sought after in today's technology landscape.

We wish you the best of luck on your AWS Certified Developer journey. Your dedication, commitment, and continuous learning will undoubtedly lead you to success. Now, go ahead, practice, learn, and conquer the AWS Certified Developer exam!

www.ingramcontent.com/pod-product-compliance
Lightning Source LLC
LaVergne TN
LVHW082354200926
848481LV00012B/3558